Gunrunner

Gunrunner

by

Mario Oliveira

Keith Knotek

Burning Bulb
PUBLISHING

Burning Bulb Publishing
P.O. Box 4721
Bridgeport, WV 26330
www.burningbulbpublishing.com

On Death

*So, live your life that the fear of death can never
enter your heart. Trouble no one about their
religion; respect others in their view, and demand
that they respect yours. Love your life, perfect your
life, beautify all things in your life. Seek to make
your life long and its purpose in the service of your
people. Prepare a noble death song for the day
when you go over the great divide.*

*When it comes your time to die, be not like those
whose hearts are filled with the fear of death so
that when their time comes, they weep and pray
for a little more time to live their lives over again in
a different way. Sing your death song and die like a
hero going home.*

~ Tecumseh, Warrior Chief of the Shawnee

CONTENTS

Author's Note

When I wrote an autobiographical book in 2020, I never had any plans to write another book. Then in July 2021 entered Mario Oliveira, who said he wanted someone to write his story. I thought to myself, *everybody has a story, but I'm just not looking to take on anything else – besides, I only write about topics I'm passionate about, and I am not a "ghostwriter."* At the time, my first book was being turned into a movie, and production was about to begin. I was also getting ready to go back to one of our state universities to teach a few classes for the upcoming semester.

My old "cop nature" was cynical and skeptical of anything and everyone I met. However, I learned in post-retirement that God has a purpose for everyone and to be a little more open-minded. Mario proceeded to tell me his story as I sank back into the sofa's cushions with amusement. I listened intently, giving no thought as to what I would say next, and I felt myself being moved by Mario's words. Something within me began to awaken as he described some definitive moments in his life and career.

By the end of our conversation, I told Mario that his story was truly remarkable and that God had blessed him in a very personal and intimate way. As a result, I did not immediately commit to writing this work, and I asked Mario to let me "percolate" on it for a bit. I first wanted to pray on it for some kind of affirmation that this would be pleasing to God in carrying out His purpose. I also wanted to discuss it with my wife to ensure she would support me as I devoted time away from her to complete this project.

I prayed, spoke with my wife, and processed what Mario and I had discussed. Mario also sent me a recorded interview with his trauma center surgeon, Dr. David King, and himself. After watching the video and being receptive to that "still small voice" of the Holy Spirit, I resoundingly decided to write Mario's story. His is a powerful case study of modern-day miracles, and I knew I needed to become involved in it. I became acutely aware that this story was exceptional, and people needed to hear it.

Every day and all around us, an unseen combat rages on. It is invisible, yet we can sometimes feel it in every aspect of our lives, especially for those working in law enforcement. It is a spiritual battle – a war between good and evil. An act of the utmost evil almost ended Mario's earthly life forever. However, God had other plans to use Mario and his story for His (God's) glory and purpose. Our enemy is evil itself, but in this case, good wins and hails victorious over wickedness.

Although this book is about the life of Mario Oliveira, it is truly a tale of two men whose paths crossed on one cold night in November 2010 – Mario and Dr. (COL) David King. These two men came from different parts of the country and had very different backgrounds. They had never known each other until they met in what would later become a miracle affirmed and the start of a close brotherly bond and friendship.

Who would have thought that an east coast guy would connect with this west coast guy and collaborate on a book? But, we're here to tell you that is precisely what occurred. God planted a seed in Mario's heart, and through divine providence, He presented me with an opportunity to work with two extraordinary men in telling this fantastic story. As a result, I formed an unbreakable bond with Mario Oliveira and Dr. David King, who I now call my brothers.

The content in this book was compiled over ten months in which I interviewed Mario Oliveira, Dr. David King, and a confidential informant named *"Leon"* remotely via video. We also had several opportunities to meet in person. Capturing Mario's words and raw emotion was essential to tell the whole story, and I didn't want to mess it up. Much of the dialogue in this book is directly quoted. Unless otherwise specified, most of the chapters in this chronicle were written as if Mario was the "storyteller." All parties involved felt it was important to convey the rawness to the readers of what really happened. So, yes, there is some colorful language in the book. What makes this story so spectacular is that every bit of it is true. The events discussed in the book have been validated, attested to by credible witnesses, and are well-documented in medical and law enforcement records and news media sources.

One never knows when, how, or in what capacity God will reveal Himself to us. But when He does, watch out because you will never be the same again.

–Keith R. Knotek

Statements of Support

Detective Mario Oliveira's story has needed to be told, and Keith Knotek is the perfect author to tell it. Gunrunner is not a piece of fiction but a gripping rollercoaster account of extraordinary real people. Punctuated by illustrations of bravery, resilience, faith, despair, and the human spirit's power, each chapter builds deliberately upon the last, steering the reader towards a dramatic crescendo on that ill-fated evening of November 2nd, 2010.

Carefully setting the stage for their eventual meeting, Knotek explores Dr. David King's and Mario Oliveira's early lives and careers in poignant detail. Knotek so lucidly portrays their parallel desire to be of service to others that it feels unmistakably predestined when Mario's path crosses with Dr. King's. Shared values, an irrepressible spirit, and past exposure to violence and pain created the perfect storm of conditions for their life-and-death first meeting and friendship, described so beautifully here.

Immediate takeaways from this book are that vulnerability and authentic human connection can heal even the most broken parts of us; no matter what we encounter, there's always hope for a better day. Anyone engaged in law enforcement, the military, and healthcare would benefit from reading Gunrunner; however, the book appeals to a much broader audience as the experiences and lessons are universally felt. Gunrunner is the ultimate testament to the power of faith to sustain and bring us through the darkest of times and provide purpose and healing in its aftermath.

–Sarah E. Abbott, Ph.D., LSW
Director
William James College Center for
Crisis Response and Behavioral Health

On November 2, 2010, I proudly had the honor of serving the Somerville, Massachusetts Police Department as the Chief of Police. As those in Law Enforcement can attest, the Chief's position is the pinnacle of a police officer's career as they rise through the ranks. But, unfortunately, with this honor comes the responsibility of being on call twenty-four hours a day/seven days a week.

On November 2, 2010, while on my way home to vote, I received a phone call from one of my detectives. Of course, this type of phone call is the kind of call nobody wants to receive. The detective told me that there was an officer-involved shooting, and Detective Mario Oliveira was shot multiple times at point-blank range. He was transported to the Massachusetts General Hospital, but his condition is critical.

Thankfully, I was in my unmarked cruiser and immediately responded to the M.G.H. code three! As I arrived at the hospital, the paramedics were removing the stretcher from the back of the ambulance, surrounded by several Somerville Police Officers who were part of the ambulance escort.

As hundreds of police officers, friends, and family members remained at the hospital waiting to hear about Mario's condition, I attempted to maintain my composure and be a strong show of support for the Oliveira family and my officers.

Detective Mario Oliveira was more to me than just a "Cops Cop." He is one of the most dedicated, committed, compassionate, and highly decorated police officers in the history of the Somerville Police Department. He was a consummate professional who desired to be a police officer and did what he had to do to reach his goal and dream.

I witnessed Mario's dedication, compassion, and desire to be the best police officer he could be and somebody who greatly appreciated what it meant to be a loving son, brother, husband, and dad.

On November 2, 2010, his dream, career, and, most importantly, his family's life were shattered while performing his duties as a Somerville Police Detective and member of the A.T.F. Task Force. Mario almost made the ultimate sacrifice as a police officer after being shot multiple times and dying on the table during surgery. However, if it were not for Doctor King and his staff at M.G.H., this story would have a more tragic ending.

However, this story is about a police officer who took a tragedy in his career and life; and made it an opportunity to change the lives of others. Mario became the president of Concern of Police Survivors (C.O.P.S.), an organization that helps families after the death of a police officer in their family. He also started an organization for Violently Injured Police Officers (V.I.P.O) who were injured and disabled in the line of duty.

Detective Mario Oliveira has received commendations, accolades, and awards that any police officer would be proud to receive. These commendations from Federal, State, Local, and other organizations, including the Somerville Police Department, are greatly appreciated. But, Mario will tell you that he would trade every one of these commendations to be a police officer again and not watch the pain and suffering his family went through, especially his wife and children, during this tragedy.

I am proud of what Mario did as a Somerville Police Officer, Detective, member of the A.T.F. Task Force, and continuing to help others in need. He is truly one of Somerville's finest, a true hero, but more importantly, he is a family man and my friend.

−Michael Cabral
Chief of Police (Ret.)
Somerville, Massachusetts Police Department

"Gunrunner" is a fantastic book that is a must-read for all who protect and serve. In other words, everyone. It is an intense true story of a young detective who took the oath to protect the citizens of Somerville, Massachusetts, and what he ran up against day to day. It was a devastating journey for this Police Officer to survive the unthinkable and living to write about it. An emotional roller coaster from Chapter to Chapter that results in Faith, Belief, and Hope.

–Eileen Goodick
Director
Massachusetts Police Training Center,
Plymouth Police Academy

Having walked, sometimes crawled through the painful terrain of grief, suicidal ideation, and trauma, I could relate to so much in Mario's story. The truth is I had no idea how incredibly tough it would be to find life on the other side of losing a husband and daughter in a car crash 18 years ago.

Mario's story is one of strength and resilience. Together Keith and Mario share the highs and lows that so many face today while navigating their own complex issues. What is bone-chilling and compelling is the way that God shows up in his story. Reading his story deepened my faith in the God who wants you to know- He sees you and loves you. This is a story I will share far and wide.

–Jennifer Tracy
Life Coach, Author
From the Deepest Darkness to the Light of Hope,
Inside the Mind of Suicide

I was honored to have read the manuscript for *Gunrunner*. I am not a person who reads many books, and if I feel the book is not keeping my attention, I put it down and walk away. However, I started reading the manuscript and finished the complete manuscript in its entirety! This true story had my full attention from start to finish and left me wanting to know more. What Mario Oliveira had been through and how he lives his life now is truly unique. Dr. David King is also a stellar man and physician. The journey that Mario Oliveira and Dr. King have been on and their relationship with each other after all both have been through is genuinely movie-worthy. This story touched my heart and had me on the edge of my seat.

–Sean Percy
Senior Staff Officer
Massachusetts Police Training Center,
Plymouth Police Academy

Foreword

Gunrunner is a remarkable true story that almost never came to fruition. Fortunately, for the protagonist, Mario Oliveira, made it back from the great dark chasm to tell his story of faith, courage, fortitude, and the will to survive. Mario's life chronicle has merit in standing alone as an amazing testament of faith. However, one of the most astounding elements in this written account is the fact that the other key figure, Dr. (COL) David King, had a supernatural type of experience of his own years later.

The story of Mario's struggle is one that brings hope to everyone who has been down the same path after experiencing combat or a critical incident. Mario found the answer to post-traumatic stress through his relationship with God and with the support of his family and friends. Some may have turned to other solutions like *the drink* or even more extreme measures, but not Mario.

Dr. (COL) David King is a warrior in the true sense of the word's meaning. He could have certainly focused on his civilian career as a trauma surgeon but instead made the personal choice to do more by being commissioned into the United States Army Reserve. He opted to take his skills to the battlefield, where he was introduced to the realities of war. His abilities and proficiency in his field ultimately earned him a selection into our /armed Forces special operations.

Writing can be tricky, even for authors who do it all of the time. However, Keith Knotek does a beautiful job of detailing the events that took place and capturing the raw emotion of what happens before, during, and after a critical incident. For some soldiers and police officers, the harsh realities of combat and the bitter daily grind on the streets can take a toll on one's psyche and mental health. However, these great Americans have shown the world what they are made of – grit, tenacity, and duty.

David King, Mario Oliveira, and Keith Knotek have all experienced violence, carnage, and evil because of the nature of their current or previous professions. But all three men have had spiritual experiences and know there is an eternal light in this murky world. They could have succumbed to the darkness but instead pushed forward and have tried to make the world a better place by leading the way and collaborating on this beautiful book.

The book begs the question, is there a god? I indeed believe there is a God and that he cares for our well-being, expects us to fight evil and protect the oppressed, and watches over us. First, however, ask yourself the question and then answer it for yourself after reading this story.

With wars currently waging in Eastern Europe and Southwest Asia, and during a time when things seem so unclear and convoluted, it's nice to read about actual events that do not include politics, racial bias, and political correctness. This book hits the mark in that it is a genuine human-interest story that contains all of the elements of faith, true crime, action, compassion, and revelation.

–David L. Grange
Brigadier General, USA (Ret.)
Author of *Air-Mech-Strike:*
Asymmetric Maneuver Warfare
for the 21st Century

MG David L. Grange

Biography

David L. Grange is a retired United States Army brigadier general. He served with the 101st Airborne Division during the Vietnam War. He was later assigned to Delta Force, commanding a squadron during the invasion of Grenada and was deputy commander during the Gulf War. His last command was of 1st Infantry Division before he retired in 1999.

Grange was commissioned as an infantry officer in December 1969, and first saw significant combat action as a second lieutenant assigned to the 101st

Airborne's "Lima" Ranger company in Vietnam in 1970.In 1974, Grange completed Flight training and subsequently served with the 158th Aviation Brigade. In 1981 Grange completed the grueling British SAS Course at Hereford, England then attended the Marine Corps Command and Staff College.

After multiple assignments Grange was then assigned as special-operations officer with Special Operations Command, Washington, D.C. in 1989. He attended the National War College and returned to Fort Bragg in June 1990 as deputy commander of Delta Force, in which job he commanded a task force during Desert Storm.

From July 1991 to July 1993, Grange commanded the 75th Ranger Regiment. He then served as deputy commanding officer of United States Army Special Operations Command. After his selection as a general officer, he served as both Assistant Div. Commander for support and maneuver in the 3rd Infantry Division at Warner Barracks in Bamberg, Germany.

In 1997, Grange returned to Germany and took command of the 1st Infantry Division and Task Force Eagle in Bosnia, where he was responsible for U.S. forces and operations in North Macedonia and Kosovo during the Yugoslav Wars. Grange retired from active-duty service in 1999.

Grange then led a group of Army officers who wrote a book on improving force structure; *Air-Mech-Strike: Asymmetric Maneuver Warfare for the 21st Century*. He later served president of the McCormick Foundation in Chicago, and was inducted into the U.S. Army Ranger Hall of Fame in 2005.

Grange later founded Osprey Global Solutions, a consulting firm and government contractor that offers logistics, intelligence, medical, security training, armament sales, financial forensics, construction and other services. He is also the CEO of Osprey Armament, which develops specialized weapons and conducts beginner to advanced training at the Osprey Training Center in Council, North Carolina.

Some of Grange's military awards and decorations include: three Silver Star Medals; the Defense Superior Service Medal; three Legions of Merit; two Bronze Star Medals; two Purple Heart Medals; two Defense Meritorious Service Medals; three Meritorious Services Medals; and four Air Medals.

General Grange is a Knight Commander in the Military and Hospitaller Order of St. Lazarus of Jerusalem.

Grange lives in North Carolina with his wife Holly.

Acknowledgments

I want to dedicate this book in memory of my late grandmother Julia Lima (February 17, 1919 – March 15, 1984), who undoubtedly is my guardian angel. Julia Lima was a woman of deep faith, a great mother and grandmother who was a fierce protector of her family. I was also her favorite grandson, so I've been told.

I would be remiss if I did not acknowledge our Lord and Savior Jesus Christ, who, with His divine providence, sent my guardian angel to visit me at the hour of my death on November 2, 2010. My guardian angel gave me hope and faith that I would survive my horrific shooting ordeal. My parents are devout Catholics who believe in God and the power of prayer.

I publicly thank my parents, Humberto and Margaret Oliveira, for raising six wonderful boys who have grown up to be successful fathers, sons, and husbands. My parents instilled a tremendous work ethic in all their children, which enabled us to strive and succeed in anything we did. I am deeply sorry for giving them some major scares over the last ten years.

I would also like to acknowledge my wife, Christy, who has quietly endured so much mental anguish from my medical setbacks and putting up with my hectic work schedule. Christy picked up the slack at home when I was in the hospital. She is a hard worker and a phenomenal mother to our three young boys.

To my three boys, you are my world. I want to thank Andrew, 14; Tyler, 10; and Luke, 5, who have remained resilient throughout my medical setbacks. My boys stayed strong while they watched their dad being carted off into an ambulance and when they visited me in the hospital. My boys are my world, and I pray that they possess my grit and will to live. I know in my heart that they will be successful, brave men in the future.

I want to acknowledge Dr. David King, the trauma surgeon who saved me the night I was shot. He has become one of my closest friends, and I genuinely believe that everything happens for a reason. Dr. King and his team were there that night to receive me in the Emergency Room and ultimately save my life. Without Dr. King, I wouldn't be here to share my story. I would also like to thank Dr. King for his service to our country.

I would also like to acknowledge two exceptional men who touched my life profoundly. I want to thank Donald Kennedy and Glenn Browning, my former bosses at my current employment, The New England State Police Information Network (NESPIN). Both

Don and Glenn took a chance in hiring me in 2016. By all accounts, I should not have been the one selected for the Eastern Massachusetts Law Enforcement Coordinator position. There were far many more qualified candidates they could have chosen. However, with a little bit of help from God, who I pray to daily, and the kind hearts these men possessed, they chose me as their new Eastern Mass Law Enforcement Coordinator. I promised both Don and Glenn that I would never allow them to regret hiring me.

Sadly, Don Kennedy passed away in April 2022 from an illness. In my opinion, this remarkable man did not have an opportunity to properly enjoy his retirement after dedicating over 40 years of his life to Law Enforcement. I know that Don is now at peace in heaven and no longer suffering. Likewise, I am happy to report that Glenn Browning lives his best life in Utah, doing what he loves: skiing, hiking, and spending quality time with his wonderful wife, Lynne. I will be forever grateful for Don Kennedy and Glenn Browning, who gave me a chance to be back in law enforcement, allowing me to take care of my family financially. I can't begin to tell you how my current job has saved me in so many ways.

Additionally, I would like to thank my partner and coauthor, Keith Knotek, who has been my confidant and brother for the last ten months as we cowrote this book. I am grateful Keith found time to help me share my message of hope and faith. I have made a friend for life, no doubt. Keith and his beautiful wife Lily are now part of my family.

Last but not least, to my brothers and sisters in Blue. I see you. I watch you suffer quietly when we lose a brother or sister to the criminals on the street. I see you comfort the victims that will seemingly haunt your dreams and never seem to be in short supply. I see you patrol the cities and towns with one mission, to protect and serve. I see you stand together to serve as the thin blue line. I see you confront the evil that others pretend does not exist. I see you, appreciate you, applaud you, and most importantly, I thank you.

–Mario L. Oliveira

Introduction
November 2nd – the night I died.

The fear of death follows from the fear of life. A man who lives fully is prepared to die at any time.

~ Mark Twain

It was a calm and clear November night in Somerville. Aside from the usual light pollution from the urban landscape and city streetlights, I can remember seeing stars in the night sky. It was general election night in the town on November 2nd, and there were a lot of cops working extra duty assignments keeping law and order at the polling stations. I happened to be working on my normal task force assignment that night. Other than the fact that there would be many people on the streets that evening due to the election, I figured it would be a quiet and uneventful shift. I wore civilian attire and had my badge stowed on a neck chain type badge holder underneath my shirt. I usually didn't wear my bulletproof vest as a task force detective as I did on patrol. But, of course, I'd put it on if we were going to serve an arrest warrant or hit a house on a search warrant.

My partner Brian Hudson and I decided to take a drive-by Matthew Kramer's mother's house on Gibbens Street. The kid skipped town and knew he'd be arrested if we found him. So, what would the chances be of him actually being in Somerville on election night? As we pulled onto Gibbens Street from Benton Street, we looked and saw Kramer's red Honda Accord parked in front of his mother's house. Holy crap, he's there! Yes, Matt's car was parked in front of his mom's house. I need to set up on the house and throw a plan together – this I did not expect!

I called my lieutenant Joe McCain and Sergeant Jerry Reardon to come over to my location. I told them to meet me on the sidewalk at Gibbens Street and Central Street because Matt Kramer, a wanted felon, was in the area. The plan we ultimately came up with was that when I saw Matt go to his vehicle, I would run up behind him and get him "proned out" on the ground. Brian will come around with our unmarked police car and "bumper lock" Matt's car so he can't get in and drive away. Essentially, bumper locking is putting the front bumper of our police car against the front bumper of Matt's car. My lieutenant and my sergeant were going to be my backup. I'm going to cuff him up and cart him off to jail. *Yep, sounds like a solid plan; let's do it!*

Oh, no! Matt made it to his car before I could get to him. I started running over to him. As soon as he started his car's engine, I opened his car door, grabbed him around his throat, and put my pistol to his head. I visibly displayed my badge over my shirt, and I started giving him commands, "Get out of the car; you're under arrest. Get out of the car!" I noticed that he straightened his legs out and pressed his feet onto the car's floorboard, making it very difficult for me to pull him out of the vehicle. At one point, Matt started repeatedly screaming, "Fucking shoot me!" "Fucking shoot me!" I remember thinking to myself, *shit, I've got to get him out of this car.*

My sergeant ran up to the vehicle on the passenger side of Matt's car and yelled, "Mario!" I looked at him to see what he wanted. But when I looked back down at Matt, all I could see was the blinding light of muzzle flash through the darkness. The sound of gunfire shattered the calmness of the quiet night. I was blown backward and knocked down on my ass onto the asphalt. *Oh, my God! I've been shot,* I thought to myself.

Then the dark street lit up with brilliant flashes of light. There was a gunfight going on. I did my best to get into the fight. But as I tried to raise my pistol to aim at my assailant, I couldn't move, no matter how hard I tried to get it to budge. That little bastard had shot me in the forearm of my gun hand, and it was totally disabled.

Brian had the foresight to drag me across the street and away from Matt's vehicle so that I wouldn't be in the crossfire. I could hear all of the chaos going on around me. Then I heard Matt's mother shouting, "That's my son, that's my son," and my Lieutenant, Joe McCain, yelling, "Get back in the house!" At that point, I became fully aware that I had been shot and was losing a lot of blood. As I looked up at the stars in the sky, I became so scared. I began to cry but deliberately controlled and slowed down my breathing so that I would not hyperventilate. I needed to minimize the blood flow so that I didn't bleed out that roadside.

At that moment, it was like a switch got flipped in my mind. I went from feeling shear panic into a state of peace. I remembered playing hide and seek and street hockey as a kid on Rush Street. My brain tuned out all of the commotions around me and was preparing me to go to a beautiful place. Tonight would be the night that I die.

Chapter 1
Humble Beginnings

God always gives a great blessing to humble beginnings than to those that start with the chiming of bells.

~ St. Vincent de Paul

I was born in Saint Michael, part of the Azores, a chain of islands and part of Portugal. Saint Michael is the largest of the islands and is nicknamed *Ilha Verde,* or "The Green Island." The island itself is only about 287 square miles of landmass, and of course, Portuguese is the national language spoken there. Ponta Delgada is the capital and the largest city within the Azores. The Azores are also Europe's westernmost region.

The year was 1968, and the world was not without strife. *First, the Tet Offensive* was carried out by U.S. forces in Vietnam and resulted in the highest casualty toll of the Vietnam War to date at the time. Then, on April 5, 1968, Dr. Martin Luther King, Jr. was assassinated by an unstable and unemployed army veteran. Finally, two months later, an assassin's bullet found its mark and killed U.S. Senator Robert F. Kennedy.

In November 1968, Richard M. Nixon was proclaimed the champion in the general election beating out the Democratic candidate Hubert Humphrey and the independent candidate George C. Wallace for President of the United States. Fortunately, the tumultuous year ended positively as three astronauts aboard the Apollo 8 spacecraft—Bill Anders, Frank Borman, and Jim Lovell—became the first humans to orbit the moon. After speeding to over 24,000 mph to break free of Earth's gravitational pull, Apollo 8 circled the moon ten times that Christmas Eve, attaining the latest U.S. achievement in the "Space Race" with the Soviet Union.

Up to that year in the country of my birth, Portugal had already been living under authoritarian regimes for 42 years. For 35 of those years, the people were governed under the tight grip of the Estado Novo regime led by the autocrat António de Oliveira Salazar. However, in September 1968, things slowly began to change when Salazar tripped and fell on his head. An operation to remove a blood clot in his brain was performed, but he relapsed and was left in a coma during his recovery. Salazar was subsequently replaced by Marcelo Caetano, who promoted economic growth and made some social improvements.

My family was neither wealthy nor privileged. But we all had an intense devotion to family and a solid work ethic. My parents worked for everything they had and were no strangers to "burning the midnight oil." My dad, Humberto Oliveira, was born on the island of Saint Michael in 1942. He came from a family with 13 children – seven boys and six girls. My father worked on a farm from sunrise to sunset like his father. He worked the land, raised corn, tended to the vineyard, and operated a dairy farm when he became an adult. It has been said that farming fosters good character traits and a rigid work ethic. Self-reliance, diligence, fortitude, and patience are crucial traits and qualities in agriculture.

Some of my earliest and fondest childhood memories were riding beside my dad on a horse and carriage and delivering milk all over the green island. When I think of it, I can recall the scent of freshly cut grass and the pungent odor of horse manure in my mind as if I was reliving those events today. Those were simpler times, and I knew nothing of the political strife or the economic situation in Portugal at that time. I had everything I needed – food, clothing, and shelter. Life would not become more complicated for me until later on, when my entire life would experience new people, places, and things.

My mother was also born on the island in 1942 as Margaret Lima to my grandfather Joao Lima and my grandmother Julia Lima. Mom had six siblings – three brothers and three sisters. Early on, mom learned from my grandmother how to manage a household and be a homemaker.

Traditionally, the women cleaned the house and cooked for the men who worked the land and tended to the farm all day. My parents were not afraid to get their hands dirty or use "elbow grease" to accomplish their tasks. That trait was passed down to them from generation to generation and was instilled in me as a little boy. So, the "daily grind" was familiar to me, and I just assumed I'd become a farmer like my dad and grandfather.

However, things were about to change for my family and me when I was almost four years old. Due to the fact my dad's parents and his brother had already relocated to the Eastern Seaboard of the United States for a better way of life, he began to consider following in their footsteps. Finally, the pivotal moment had arrived as my parents, siblings, and I had landed at Logan Airport in Boston in 1972 with the clothing on our backs and very few material possessions. However, my parents had hope, faith, and a promise for a more desirable quality of life.

São Miguel (St. Michael) Island, The Azores, Portugal

Chapter 2
A New Beginning

Train up a child in the way he should go,
and when he is old, he will not depart from it.
(NKJV)

~ Proverbs 22:6

Now I'm a four-year-old immigrant kid from Portugal in a completely foreign place to me. I didn't know anyone except for my dad's parents and my uncle. I couldn't speak a lick of English, and I wore clothing that was different from all of the other kids' attire. We came from the countryside and moved into my grandfather's basement on Curtis Street in what was an urban jungle in the heart of Somerville, Massachusetts. I was used to seeing cattle, green pastures, subtropical forests, fields of grain, and vineyards. The greater Boston area had none of those things. My new surroundings consisted of wall-to-wall buildings, traffic, asphalt, and sidewalks. However, there was a reason my parents brought us here.

If we're lucky, we will ultimately acquire our parent's good character traits and emulate their good qualities. I was blessed to inherit all of those things from my mom and dad. My parents were and still are devout Roman Catholics. I was raised in the church as a youngster and attended Sunday mass with my mom and dad. So, even though I was scared to death in my foreign surroundings, I could feed off my parent's hope, optimism, perseverance, loyalty, faith in God, and family love. I should also mention that they were also very strict with my siblings and me, so if one of us got out of line or started whining about something, they would let us know and would make us toe the line.

We eventually moved out of my grandfather's home into an apartment on Glen Street that belonged to my Uncle Manny, my father's older brother. Our neighborhood was multi-ethnic and consisted of a melting pot of Italian, Irish, and Portuguese immigrants. So, there were various languages spoken by the parents and elders of the kids I grew up with. I started kindergarten at East Somerville Community School, where I learned English as a second language. The school was just a short walk from home. So, I walked to and from school every day. I excelled in most subjects except for math. My elementary school experience was my first start at assimilating to the "American way of life."

I began to make friends, and we would get together and play on Rush Street, which was just adjacent to our school. Our after-school activities consisted of taking part in many games of hide-and-seek, Relievo, and tag. As I got older, we added street hockey to our repertoire of physical activities. When it started getting dark, I knew I needed to make the short trek from Rush Street to my home on Glen Street for dinner, or I would not hear the end of it from my mother. My buddies and I participated in a lot of innocent fun. The worst thing we ever did was "egging" a few houses on Halloween. My time spent on Rush Street was some of the best moments of my young life. I remember those times so vividly and with great fondness.

By this time, my dad was working at a glue factory in Norwood, Massachusetts – a job he had held for 40 years. My mom was the primary homemaker, food prepper, house cleaner, and grocery shopper. My father used to leave the house around 6:00 AM to commute to his job at the glue factory. Dad would get off work from the glue factory, come home and eat something, and leave the house by 6:00 p.m. with my mom to clean office buildings at night. I often accompanied my parents to their job after finishing my homework. I helped them clean the offices by emptying the trash and taking out the garbage from all three floors. My dad vacuumed, and mom cleaned the bathrooms. This routine went on five nights a week – Monday through Friday.

After my elementary school experience, I went on to attend Southern Junior High School, which was located on the corner of Summer Street and Putnam Street – about a mile and a half from our home. The school was a beautiful red brick, three-story building that was constructed in the early 1900s. It used to take up the whole block but was eventually torn down in the late 1980s. Now, the old building site has been turned into a dog park.

Not to sound cliché or like my parents, but I used to walk 30-minutes every day to and from school. I did the hike, and it didn't matter if there was freezing sleet, snow, rain, or a zombie apocalypse. My siblings and I did not ditch school like some of the other kids. I did very well and excelled throughout my primary and secondary school career, except for mathematics. Numbers and equations were not my friends! However, I loved history and received excellent grades in the subject.

I hung out with other like-minded kids who had the same drive to try to do well in school. Our moral compass was pretty strong, too, and we had a good sense between right and wrong. Those values and work ethic were instilled in me by my parents when I was old enough to crawl on the floor. So, I knew, even at such a young age, that hard work and education would be the key to my success as I plodded along my new course as a Portuguese immigrant in America. Another motivating factor to excel in school was that I didn't want to shame my family name or suffer the consequences from my parents if I slacked off.

When I first arrived in the U.S. I didn't dress like the other kids. Instead, I wore the "old world" clothing of a child from southwestern Europe. But by the time I hit junior high school, I began to dress more like my classmates. I made many friends who helped me assimilate into my new way of life. My English got better and better, and my parents would take me shopping for more mainstream clothing for an American kid. Because we weren't wealthy by any means, my parents would purchase my clothes on a layaway plan – buy now, but make payments until paid in full. We did what we had to do, but I learned to live within my means.

I started loving my new life in my new country. There was so much more opportunity here than just farming and raising a family. I'm certainly not saying there is anything wrong with farming; it is an honorable and necessary trade. But I definitely knew I wanted something different for myself and also desired to raise a family of my own someday. I started feeling comfortable in my own skin, in stark contrast to how I felt when I first arrived in Boston with my family.

Somerville, Massachusetts

Chapter 3
The Learning Continues

*Good habits formed at youth
make all of the difference.*

~ Aristotle

When I was about 14 years old, I developed a real fascination with law enforcement and the police. The uniforms, the cars with their blue lights and sirens, and the job in general just intrigued me. I knew that I didn't want to grow up and work in a tedious office job. However, watching all of the cop shows of the day on television swayed me towards wanting to go into law enforcement. The men and women in law enforcement have a real mission and purpose - I just knew that I wanted to become a part of it someday.

Also, at the age of 14, I graduated junior high school and moved on to attend Somerville High School. I continued to get good grades all through high school, except for, you guessed it – mathematics! I made the varsity soccer team and also played hockey on an inner-city league team while maintaining an above-average grade point average (GPA). I stayed swamped all through high school but was able to regulate a healthy semblance of balance in my life.

I met my first sweetheart, Michelle, while attending Somerville High School. I was already a high school senior and had my driver's license by this time. Michelle was a beautiful girl and was a year younger than me. I took her to my senior prom, and we were inseparable during the time we dated. I got along well with her parents, and for a fleeting moment, I thought she could *be "the one."* But it wasn't meant to be—we just kind of drifted apart and went our separate ways after I graduated high school.

I previously mentioned helping my parents clean office buildings at night. Because I already had experience, I was able to get an afterschool job of my own, cleaning an office building, the John F. Kennedy (JFK) Federal Building in Boston. I'd catch the train at Sullivan Square every night after school and travel into Boston. After arriving in Boston, I would walk to the JFK building, which consists of twin 26-story high-rise towers and a low, four-story building. My area of responsibility was the huge cafeteria located on the second floor. I used to fold and stack about 500 chairs in the cafe and would take a dry mop to the floor. Then I'd wet mop the floor and wait for it to dry. Finally, I'd unstack the chairs and put them back in their places. And yes, I emptied and took out the trash. I used to sign over my paychecks to my parents because that's what any good son would do, right?

I graduated from Somerville High School in 1987 with a high GPA – I made the Honor Roll. So, now what? By this time, I was no stranger to hard work. I didn't want to go into farming or do a boring office job. So, what did I do? I got a job at a bank. That's right, I walked into Somerset Savings Bank near my house and asked if they were hiring. I knew most of the tellers who worked there because that was where my family and I did our banking. The manager knew me and told me to put in an application to become a teller, and I gladly obliged.

My first job at the bank was as a teller. I later got moved up into a position as a customer service representative and subsequently earned a spot in our loan department as a consumer loan officer. I liked working there, and I got along well with everyone. I got the feeling that my supervisors and coworkers also enjoyed working with me. But, since I was not attending college, I felt the need to be productive during my off time from the bank.

About a year into working for the bank, I decided to get a second job. I got hired at Delta Airlines as an aircraft load agent or "ALA." Essentially, I was the agent in charge of making sure items were loaded where they should be for weight and balance and having the responsibility of getting the plane out on time. I also ensured that the aircraft assigned to my team was serviced for arrival and departing flights and oversaw all ramp operations in my immediate work area.

I worked my two jobs concurrently from 1988 to 1997. My routine was to work my dayshift at the bank until about 3:00 PM. I'd then commute into Boston to Logan International Airport, where I'd change out of my business casual clothing into my Delta Airlines uniform. Then, finally, I'd head out to the flight line and work from 5:00 PM to 1:00 AM.

When I was 22 years old, I decided that I was going to become a United States citizen. For all intents and purposes, I was an American. I dressed like an American, worked as an American, and talked like an American. I filled out the Application for Citizenship and went to the Boston Immigration Office. I took the written test and was interviewed by an immigration and naturalization officer. I wanted this distinguishment badly!

Finally, I was invited to the historical building at Faneuil Hall to take the U.S. Citizenship Oath of Allegiance. What a proud day that was for my family and me. Even though I was not financially wealthy, I felt rich and prosperous. This symbolic act was one of my ways of saying thank you to the country that has given me so much. I knew this act of gratitude would eventually open other doors for me.

The cycle of working my two jobs repeated itself five days a week for almost nine years until a significant pivotal moment changed everything for me.

Chapter 4
Carpe Diem

When a defining moment comes along, you define the moment, or the moment defines you.

~ Kevin Costner

The year was 1997, and my brother John, who is four years younger than me, was in the police academy. He had been hired by our hometown police department Somerville PD as a police officer, and I was still working two jobs. Finally, John graduated from the police academy. I remember it as if it was yesterday. We had a graduation party for him at my parent's house. I recall John coming home in his midnight blue police uniform – the badge, the hat; the royal blue stripe going down both pant legs; and the shiny black shoes and leather gear. I wanted what he had! My goal was to become a cop someday, and my brother had realized my dream – he made it! I was so damned pleased with what he had accomplished and so very proud to be John's brother.

If my brother can do it, I can too. After all, we're both from the same family and have the same background and values. What is stopping me? Why did I wait so long? I decided that I was no longer going to wait to fulfill my dream – it was my destiny to become a police officer. I decided then and there that I wasn't going to wait any longer – it was a defining moment.

All police officer positions were filled at that time, and they weren't hiring any more officers. So, I applied to become a 911 dispatcher and radio operator for Somerville PD. I took the test and got the job. Being hired into this position was the first step toward fulfilling my dream. I became really good at dispatching and handling 911 calls in our communications center. I was composed and level-headed while working under pressure and had a good "radio ear." I had all of the necessary skills to be a proficient and excellent dispatcher. But I still hadn't achieved my calling in life.

Here's a free geography lesson in case you didn't know that Brazil is located in South America. All South American countries are Spanish-speaking nations, right? Wrong! Brazil is the only country in South America in which Portuguese is the national language. Not too unlike the United States, languages such as Spanish, English, and other languages are spoken there, but Portuguese is the native tongue. As a result, Somerville has the highest number of Brazilians of any municipality in Massachusetts, not to neglect the European immigrants like me who also speak the language.

I was one of the only dispatchers who spoke Portuguese, and there were very few police officers in the department who spoke the language. Often, the officers would come to the station in a cruiser and pick me up from the communications center. We would drive out to a crime scene where either the victim, suspect, or witnesses only spoke Portuguese, and I would translate for the officers. That actually happened quite a bit, and I was glad to get out of the radio room and do something other than answering phones and talking on the radio.

Finally, my big break came one shift when the police chief came through the radio room. He stopped and told me that I was doing an outstanding job as a dispatcher and asked me if I was still interested in becoming a police officer. I replied with a resounding, "Yes!" He went on to say that there was a real need for another bilingual officer, more specifically, one who spoke Portuguese. He went on to say he was going to write a proposal to the city council to authorize the hiring of several more officers, including a bilingual officer. I was walking on air, but I also recalled that adage, "It ain't over 'til the fat lady sings." Just because the chief wanted to hire more officers didn't mean he would get what he asked for.

A few weeks later, I was working in the communications center on the dayshift when one of the internal phone lines rang. The chief's secretary called and summoned me up to the chief's office. I got so excited that this could be the moment I was waiting for – or did I screw up and was getting called out onto the carpet. In the two seconds it took for me to psych myself out and stop playing different scenarios in my mind, I took the walk to see the chief.

When I crossed the threshold and walked into the inner sanctum, the chief stood up, smiled, and very cordially greeted me. *"Oh, good,"* I thought to myself, *"I'm not in trouble."* The chief told me I was being hired as a police officer and that I would still be working in the communications center until I started the police academy. I couldn't believe it! It was almost surreal, but it was really happening – I was finally going to live my American dream and become a cop!

Current photo of Somerville Police Headquarters

Chapter 5
Living the Dream

"A dream doesn't become reality through magic; it takes sweat, determination, and hard work."

~ Colin Powell

Massachusetts is different than some states when it comes to police officer training and certification. Some agencies in other parts of the country have job classifications like cadet or recruit. The cadet or recruit isn't reclassified to the position of a police officer until they receive their basic training and graduate from the police academy. Everyone attending the academy has already been hired as a police officer in Massachusetts. So, in 1998, I was hired as an officer and continued to work in dispatch until my primary police academy started in 1999.

My adventure into the next chapter of life started at the Plymouth Police Academy, located near Long Pond Road and Pilgrim's Highway in Plymouth, Massachusetts. I spent five days a week there for five months with 50 other student police officers from all over eastern Massachusetts. The campus was an old school building where we participated in classroom instruction and academics. The parking lot served as our "grinder" or parade ground, where we spent countless hours drilling, marching, running, and conducting physical training (PT). As one drill instructor said, "The physical pain you experience here reminds you that you're still alive. The suffering you endure here is so that you don't have to when you hit the streets!"

So, my life, at least for five months, consisted of drills and ceremonies; doing four and five-mile runs; PT; uniform inspection; academics and testing; weapons qualification; defensive tactics; emergency vehicle operations course (EVOC), also known as defensive driving; and more PT – sometimes until you puked! There's a reason why seasoned veterans tell you to get in shape BEFORE the academy starts and not after you start. Unfortunately, some folks didn't heed that advice, and their fellow students literally had to carry them through the training. The academy staff really pumped the "leave no one behind" philosophy into us.

Academy student officers were expected to maintain a healthy lifestyle and to do all of the things that promote good health and proper physical conditioning. The following is an excerpt straight out of the academy's Student Handbook:

"The academy provides basic skills to help recruits lead a healthy lifestyle and achieve longevity with improved on-the-job perform-ance. Instructors will help recruits develop personalized plans to promote lifetime wellness habits. This includes, but is not limited

to the following: 1. nutrition 2. proper sleep & rest 3. stress management 4. maintain a healthy weight 5. Disease and injury prevention; 5. Physical fitness."

We even had to keep a nutrition journal of everything we ate. The academy staff routinely reviewed that journal to ensure we were doing everything possible to maintain and improve our physical condition.

Why am I telling you all of this information? Let me explain. I previously mentioned that my brother John had gone through the academy and was already working as a Somerville police officer. So, unbeknownst to me, John decided to call the academy staff to let them know I loved eating junk food. My poison of choice was Yodels. You may be asking yourself, *"What are Yodels?"* I will tell you that Yodels are the best thing since sliced bread. Yodels are like manna from heaven but are even better! They are an East Coast snack food similar to Ho Hos and Little Debbie's Swiss cake rolls. They are little cream-filled cakes and are packed full of all kinds of deliciousness.

One day, I was in formation and standing at attention out on the grinder when one of the drill instructors, Senior Staff Instructor (SSI) Lenny Mota, shouted, "Oliveira, front and center!" SSI Mota was a New Bedford police officer and a former

Marine. He was also very intimidating. As I reported to the front of the formation, Mota lurched forward and got in my face. The brim of his campaign hat was about one inch from my nose when he started yelling something to the effect of, "A little birdie told me you like eating junk food! Is that true?" I stated that I wasn't sure what he was referring to. He then told me, "I deprived my daughters of their lunch money today, and I bought you these," as he proceeded to pull out a 3-pack of Yodels from his pocket. "Do these look familiar," he asked. I exclaimed, "Yes, sir!" SSI Mota had me extend my arm out, and he placed the pack of Yodels in my hand. Mota went on to say that the class was going on a 4-mile run, and I was going to lead them in calling cadence. He said that I was to carry the Yodels in my hand during the entire duration of the run. If the Yodels were crushed or damaged in any way during the run, I was going to have to write a 10-page disciplinary memo to him about how and why they were destroyed.

After the group of us arrived back on campus, SSI Mota had me report to the front of the formation again. He inspected the pack of Yodels which I am proud to say were not crushed or damaged. SSI Mota said, "Oliveira, you impress me. Now you're going to yodel for the class. In fact, I want you to yodel so loud that your brother John can hear you all of the way up in Somerville!" Oh, *"that butthead, John,"* I thought to myself. What goes around comes around. So, I ended up yodeling as loud as I could as SSI Mota began to stuff my mouth with Yodels cakes. I was already exhausted and queasy from the run and almost barfed after eating the second cake. I said, "Sir, I think I'm going to puke," at which time Mota asked, "Would you like to donate your last Yodel?" I said, "Yes, sir," and another deserving student officer got to eat it. SSI Mota never called me by my name again and would only refer to me as "Yodels" from that day forward.

The academy was located about 45 miles from Somerville and our daily start time was at 0700 hours (7:00 AM), which meant I had to leave the house early and before the sun came up if I was going to be there on time. Another new boot Somerville officer also attended the academy with me – Bob Smith. But the two of us carpooled to and from the academy every day. Our routine was to drive from our homes to the Somerville Police Station. We'd leave our personal vehicles in the parking lot and would check out an old cruiser to go to Plymouth.

I usually drove, but one day I was absolutely exhausted. So, I asked Bob to drive us home while I took a little nap in the passenger seat. The last thing I needed was to stack up a Somerville police car on the highway on my way home from the academy. As Bob was driving, I didn't realize in my slumber that he was going like a bat out of hell. Apparently, a Massachusetts State Police trooper saw us speeding down the freeway, and he got close enough to see our distinctive khaki-colored uniforms. Only academy students wore khakis instead of the blue uniforms that regular officers wore. The following day when we reported for duty at the academy, we got our butts reamed. The trooper had reported us to the academy director. Because the academy staff was pumping the "working in teams" concept in us, I got in trouble, too, even though Bob was the one who was driving.

The thing about Bob was that he was a less than stellar student officer and police officer. His class standing was very low, and he got poor grades in almost everything. However, his grades were just barely good enough to pass the academy. Bob's performance out of the street wasn't great either. He was lazy, and I didn't trust him to do his job correctly. He eventually got in trouble due to his off-duty behavior and was fired. So, the issue ultimately resolved itself.

My best friend in the academy was Gordie Clark. He was a captain with the Middlesex Sheriff's office – that's right, a captain. Unlike most sheriff's departments in the country, the sheriff's offices in Massachusetts are only responsible for the county jails and serving civil process. But the Middlesex County Sheriff's Office was starting a warrant apprehension unit in which Gordie would be the team leader. Because sheriff's deputies only had basic training with a focus on corrections, Gordie had to attend our academy to receive more specialized training with a street law enforcement emphasis.

Gordie was the oldest guy in class at the age of 47. He was also the tallest, standing at the height of 6 feet and 5 inches. I was the shortest guy at 5 feet 5 inches tall. What an unlikely pair we made. But we formed a friendship and a bond that we still have to this day. Gordie was our class president. He was kind of a mentor to me as he had already worked in law enforcement. Gordie was also highly respected and a class act.

I will always remember my time at the police academy fondly. I still try to live up to our class motto – "It takes teamwork to make a dream work."

Dad, Brother John, Mario, and Mom on
Academy graduation day

Chapter 6
Let the Games Begin!

Experience is the teacher of all things.

~ Julius Caesar

I graduated from the police academy and hit the streets with my field training officer (FTO), Steve Johnson. He was about 6 feet and 8 inches tall and lean. Like Bubba Smith's fictional character in the old Police Academy movie series, the guys affectionately called him *Hightower*. I should remind you that I am only about 5 feet and 5 inches tall. So, imagine how we must have looked paired up together as a team. I learned so much about being a cop from Steve, and I am genuinely grateful to have had him as my mentor. We worked the midnight shift together. Generally speaking, cops, newspaper delivery people, and crooks are the only people out after midnight.

A month into my training Steve and I came up to the intersection of Pearl Street and Walnut Street. We came up behind a vehicle that was stopped for the red traffic signal light. Then the light turned green and cycled back to red again. The lead car didn't budge. Okay, so the light turned green again, and I got out of our patrol car. I was going to tell the driver to pull his head out of his butt and to go when the light turned green again. I walked up to the driver's side window which was rolled down. I think I heard the snoring coming from the car before making it to the window. The guy was hammered, and I didn't even have to look that hard for what ended up being my second or third driving under the influence (DUI) arrest.

Another memorable time was when Steve and I were patrolling the city, and we drove through a gas station parking lot. There was a carload of people in the lot, and the driver was eyeballing us. We were eyeballing him too. The thing about being a cop is that you develop this sixth sense that other people don't typically have. "They're up to no good," I said to Steve. He replied, "Yeah, they look like dirtbags." I called in the license plate to dispatch. As we started pulling in behind the vehicle, the car peeled out and took off at a high rate of speed.

The chase was on! I no sooner called in the plate when dispatch came back and told us the vehicle was stolen out of a neighboring jurisdiction. They were hauling ass, and I wasn't going to let that little bastard get away from us. I didn't want any innocent civilians getting in our way in the process. We went through Somerville and into Medford. Then the car chase went into Malden, Everett, Chelsea, and back into Everett again.

The suspect vehicle crashed into another car as we crossed back into Malden from Everett. Then the driver got out and began to beat feet from the scene of the crash. I chased that bastard down the street and onto the next road. I chased him over fences, walls, and through backyards. I began to close in the distance until I finally tackled him. He went down like a sack of potatoes. I was tired and out of breath. But I could still feel the adrenaline surging through my body as I got him in handcuffs.

The suspect's name was DeShawn Williams, and he liked stealing cars. I suppose everyone has a gift or a talent, and DeShawn had a real knack for jacking cars. He just couldn't help himself. DeShawn went to prison for three years on our grand theft auto (GTA) and felony pursuit case. Remember, my brother John is also a cop for the Somerville PD. The funny thing is that after DeShawn was released from prison on my case, my brother John spotted him driving another stolen car and went into pursuit of him. He caught DeShawn, and he ended up going to prison again. Folks, you just can't make this stuff up!

I completed my field training program and was released to work on my own as a solo officer. One day I was on patrol by myself and driving north on Mystic Avenue when I heard a dispatch broadcast over the radio. The dispatcher said an armed robbery had just occurred in the city of Medford, which is located just north of Somerville, and that the suspect vehicle was a white Cadillac Coupe de Ville. As I looked up Mystic Avenue, I saw a white Cadillac Coupe de Ville driving south, crossing over from Medford into Somerville.

That particular model of Cadillac wasn't popular in those days. *Holy shit,* I thought to myself, *is this the car?* I made a U-turn and got in behind the vehicle. We turned right onto westbound Temple Street. I was calling out our direction of travel over the radio and didn't want to stop the car until I had plenty of backup with me.

We seemed to be driving all over the city, and although they were heading my way, I still had no backup. The "Cadi" suddenly turned into the Star Market parking lot and was cruising at a low rate of speed. We rounded a corner and went down a dead-end in the parking lot. The Cadillac went all of the way to the end and turned around. He was now boxed in and had nowhere to go. *Shit!* We were head-to-head, and I was still by myself. *If I sit in my car and wait – I'm dead if this is the guy tries something,* I thought, *I'm going for it!*

"Show me your hands," I exclaimed as I bailed out of my cruiser with my pistol in hand! I continued to shout commands at the driver. Finally, I ran up to the driver's side window and pointed my gun at his head as I called him out of the vehicle and *proned him out* on the ground next to the car. As I was handcuffing him, I could see a female who appeared to be passed out and was slumped over to the side. I thought, *is she dead – did this guy kill her?* Then I saw the hypodermic needle sticking out of her arm, and that's when the lightbulb went on. These two idiots were *hypes* (heroin addicts), and they just did a robbery so they could score some more dope.

My backup finally arrived, but I already had the situation under control. Apparently, the other officers had a hard time getting through traffic. The major streets in Somerville are wicked busy during that time of the day. So, I stuffed the guy in the backseat of my cruiser and had the paramedics come out to the scene to check on the female, who was still passed out from slamming heroin. But it was a happy ending – no one got hurt, the girl lived, the guy went to jail for his crime, and I got to go home at the end of my shift.

One quiet, warm summer morning around 4:00 AM, I was parked underneath the Interstate 93 overpass near Fellsway. Another cruiser pulled up next to me, and it was one of the new rookies, Marcos. Now, remember I'm not the tallest guy in the world. Marcos is even shorter than me, standing at 5 feet and 3 inches tall. We were both drinking coffee, trying to pass the time away until we could go home at the end of our midnight shift.

Suddenly, the radio crackled and broke the early morning silence sending us to a possible domestic violence incident in the Mystic projects. Off we go! As we blacked out our headlights and pulled into the dimly lit alley, we could hear screaming and shouting coming from one of the apartments on the fourth floor. As we climbed the stairway to the upper floors, we could hear glass breaking inside one of the apartments. Once we located the correct apartment unit, I knocked on the door – you know, the loud annoying cop knocking on the door sound.

The door opened up slowly and partially. There was a scared-looking lady on the other side of the door. She just stared at me. I asked, "Ma'am, are you alright?" She just continued to look at me in wonder before nodding her head. I asked, "Who else is in here with you?" "My boyfriend," she replied. I asked her if I could come in and talk to her boyfriend while my partner, Marcos, spoke with her about what had happened. She opened the door all of the way as if to say *come on in*.

I found my way over to the bedroom located at the back of the apartment. When I walked inside, I saw a pretty big muscular-looking guy sitting at the foot of the bed. He looked pissed off at the world. I asked him, "Sir, are you alright?" "How did you get in here," He exclaimed. I told him that his girlfriend let us inside the humble abode.

At first, he seemed okay and that he would go along with the program. As I was pressing him for details about what had occurred, he was clearly becoming agitated and wanted nothing to do with what was happening at that moment. Suddenly, he leaped up from the bed and squared off on me with clenched fists. He stood about 6 feet and 3 inches and weighed well over 200 pounds. *Oh, shit. Here we go,* I thought to myself.

Marcos came into the bedroom when he heard all of the commotion. At that point, we tried to place him in handcuffs for our safety, but he wasn't having any of it! He began to yell and flail his arms, so we pepper-sprayed him. The pepper spray seemed to bounce off his face and did not affect him whatsoever. So, we tried to take him down to the ground, but that didn't work either.

I jumped on his back and tried to apply the *carotid sleeper hold,* but his neck was so huge I couldn't get a good grip. Marcos was trained in martial arts, and we both had a hold of this guy at one point. However, he was swinging around like a fan, and we held on to him for dear life. We looked like a couple of *dwarfs* being flung around like ragdolls by this behemoth of a man.

Marcos and I tried to call out to dispatch that we were in a fight. But we were too busy trying to get the dude under control and couldn't get to our radios. At one point during the conflict, the guy attempted to throw me out of the fourth-story bedroom window. I don't know how we did it, but we wore him out and got him into handcuffs. By the end of the melee, my nicely pressed uniform was tattered and torn, and so was Marcos's uniform. It just goes to show that the pace and tempo of a quiet shift could go from zero to 100 in less than a heartbeat.

I have so many fond memories of my time as a patrol officer. I met many good people who needed my help and many people who needed to be taken to jail by me. We, law enforcers, tend to become jaded and soured by the job because of what we see and some of the people we encounter. Over time we forget that not everyone is a predator, a wolf, or a bad person. I have always tried to keep things in their proper perspective. There are plenty of bad guys in the world, but there are a lot of good folks out there too.

Chapter 7
The One

*Love is composed of a single soul
inhabiting two bodies."*

~ Aristotle

It was a beautiful evening on March 31, 2001, and I needed to blow off some steam. So my buddy from the academy, Eric Van Ness, and I decided to go to a nightclub called the Jukebox on Tremont Street near downtown Boston. It is kind of a swanky venue located in the basement of the Marriot Hotel.

It was there that I was smitten by the most gorgeous girl in the world. She was petite with blond hair and a nice figure, and she had the most striking blue eyes I have ever seen. My cop instincts kicked in, and I could just tell that she was a *good girl – a nice girl.* She was surrounded by her "tribe" of six girlfriends, but she stood out the most to me. It was like I was looking through the dimly lit room past the other young ladies and straight into the very essence of her. I couldn't take my eyes off of this exquisite lady.

The posse of young ladies all headed out to the dance floor and began to dance together as a group. Some drunk dude who was tripping all over himself stumbled out onto the dance floor without warning.

He crashed the party and started getting close to the object of my attraction. I thought to myself, *this asshole will embarrass himself and probably trip and fall or may try to do something inappropriate with one of the girls.*

I went out onto the dance floor and made a b-line for the drunk guy who was standing too close to the blue-eyed beauty. I could tell by her facial expressions that this drunken idiot made her feel uncomfortable. So I went up to her and whispered into her ear, "If this guy tries anything funny or weird with you, I'm going to punch him out." She acknowledged me, nodded her head, and I walked away from the circle of dancing women.

I walked up to the bar to order a drink. When I turned around, I could see my *damsel in distress* looking around the room for me. Then we made eye contact. She walked up to me and asked, "Where did you go?" "Oh, I had to order a drink, but I still had my eye on you," I said. "Thank you for looking out for us. I can't stand sloppy drunks," she exclaimed. I agreed, "Neither can I." She told me her name was Christy. "Christy, I'm Mario. Can I buy you a drink," I asked? I ordered two drinks for us, and we talked and danced the night away. The more we spoke with each other I knew I wanted more!

It was getting late. As we left the Jukebox, I asked Christy if she would call to let me know she made it home safely, and she did just that! My phone rang around 2:00 AM. I answered with wonder and excitement. *Could this be the start of something new*

– *something extraordinary,* I thought? We talked about everything under the sun. I held onto every word Christy said, and I was somehow soothed just by the sound of her voice. She told me all about her family, and I told her about mine, including the fact I was an immigrant kid from Portugal. Finally, I realized it was 10:00 AM, and neither one of us had slept. Eight hours of talking on the phone was a first for me. We said our goodbyes and hung up.

Christy and I began to date. Over time I got to know her better. I loved the fact that she came from your typical *Leave It to Beaver* family. She was raised with traditional Catholic morals, values, and ethics where the family came first before all other relationships except for one – God came first. She is a kind-hearted person with a sweet disposition. She also had a good job working as a paralegal for a major Boston law firm. I began to see a future and a life with Christy later on down the road.

Three years after we had started dating, I made dinner at my house. Yes, I do cook, and I think I'm pretty good at it. But I guess it depends on who you ask. After dinner, I put on our favorite movie at the time, Serendipity, starring John Cusack and Kate Beckinsale. Yes, it's a corny romantic comedy, but what can I say? So, we're watching the film, and halfway through the movie, I pop up on the television screen during a critical moment in the dialogue. What?

That's right; I'm on the TV. Christy is looking at the screen like she's trying to wrap her head around what just happened. The me on the TV said, "Christy, I know you're probably freaked out right now. But look over to me because I have something to ask you." So, she looks over to me, who is sitting next to her on the sofa. I suddenly got off the couch and went down on one knee. I already had the ring in my hand, "Christy, will you marry me," I asked? She said yes after the initial shock wore off.

What she didn't know when the movie started was that I took the video to a friend of mine who is technically savvy. He embedded the video of me into the actual motion picture. Needless to say, I thought it was a pretty original way to propose.

Christy and I were married in a traditional Catholic marriage ceremony on November 5, 2005. I was feeling nervous, excited, scared, and exhilarated all at the same time. This sacred ritual was one of those pivotal moments I had always thought about as a kid – meeting "Mrs. Right," getting married, and eventually having children of our own.

After Christy and I were married, I remembered a Bible verse from Proverbs: "*He who finds a wife finds what is good and receives favor from the Lord* (NIV)." Yes, I was truly blessed indeed!

Brother John, Cristina (Mario's sister-in-law),
and Mario

Chapter 8
Nothing Ventured, Nothing Gained

The key to enjoying the journey is
being open to the unknown.

~ Kristine Carlson

I was earning a reputation in patrol as a proactive street cop. I took the time to stop and talk to people about whatever came to mind. Sometimes folks would just tell me about crimes and reveal things about who was committing them without me asking. I learned to listen to people and also how to be inquisitive. I couldn't believe I was getting paid by the city to drive around and talk to people. I probably would have done it for free if I didn't need the money to pay bills.

Of course, there was more to it than just chatting with community members. Sometimes I had to handle situations that no one else wanted to deal with because they didn't have the stomach for it. But I loved being a cop. Going out and making some slight difference in my community every day was more than I could ever wish or ask for. After three years of working on regular patrol, I was assigned to a uniformed street crimes unit. Members of my team and I would deal with whatever the crime trends of the week were and were tasked with investigating, enforcing, or solving whatever the problems were at the time.

There had been a recent string of breaking and enterings (B&Es) in the Greater Boston Area targeting Brazilian business owners. These criminal opportunists hit the city of Somerville numerous times, and we knew more than one individual was doing them. The jobs themselves were sophisticated. The thieves were in and out in minutes and were able to find and steal everything of value, including oversized, heavy safes. They would also hit houses owned by well-to-do Brazilian families and were pros at what they did.

Our detectives were working the case but had no actual physical evidence or lead to follow up on. It was kind of aggravating to me knowing that the community I grew up in had this rash of burglaries that were being committed against Brazilian immigrants like my family and me. Any one of us could have been the target of such nefarious deeds. The worst part was that it seemed nobody knew who was carrying out these offenses except for the criminals themselves.

One day I was driving around in my marked police cruiser, and I heard a radio call of a shoplifter detained by loss prevention officers at the Target store. I was right around the corner from the store and didn't have anything else pressing to do at that moment. So, I informed dispatch that I would handle the call and deal with the shoplifter.

When I arrived at Target, one of the loss prevention officers told me the young man who was being held took some clothing from the store and concealed it underneath his clothing. He tried to leave the store with the merchandise and was detained by store security.

I went towards the back of the store where the loss prevention office was located. When I walked into the room, this skinny kid, maybe in his late teens to early 20s, was sitting in a chair. He had dark, short-cropped hair and looked very clean cut. The braces in his mouth added to his youthful appearance. Unfortunately, his head hung low in shame, and he looked like a whipped puppy. "What's your name?" I asked. "Bruno," he replied.

I asked, "Bruno, you know why you're being detained, right?" "Yes," he said. Bruno lived in Braintree, located south of Boston and west of Weymouth. He worked for an auto mechanic service, and I wondered what he was doing stealing clothing at a store in Somerville? I received custody of the kid from the store loss prevention folks and walked him out to my cruiser to transport him to the station. I felt terrible for Bruno because my first impression was that he was a good kid who had just made a mistake.

On the way to the station, I told him, "Okay, let's see if we can figure something out that might be able to help you." I was thinking to myself, *what could this kid possibly know about the break-ins and home invasions going on in the area?* He couldn't possibly know anything because he was a squeaky-clean-looking kid and gainfully employed. Nevertheless, he had gotten himself into a bind, and I genuinely wanted to help him. *Nothing ventured, nothing gained,* I thought to myself.

"Bruno, you know there've been many break-ins in the area targeting Brazilians?" "Yeah, I know about those," he said. "Really? What's the deal with them? How are they doing it?" Bruno told me the girlfriends of all of the thieves are housekeepers. They go into people's homes and clean them. While cleaning the houses, they're also scoping out the homes and people's valuables. They go home and tell their boyfriends about safes, coin collections, guns, and other high-value property. The girlfriends know the layout of the houses, and some of them have the alarm codes of the residents with home security systems. The thieves put a plan into action based on information provided by their housekeeper-significant others and are in and out with the stolen goods in just a few minutes.

How did I not know this already? The only ones who know about the safes other than family would be people who work in the houses. I continued to interview Bruno more in-depth after we arrived at the police station. He went on to say, "They call themselves Ocean's Eleven." "Who, the crooks," I asked? "Yeah, after the movie," Bruno said.

I spoke with the store's loss prevention and asked them if they wouldn't mind not seeking charges for the theft Bruno did at the Target store. I explained the situation to them that the possibility of potentially solving multiple felony cases versus a petty misdemeanor charge outweighs the lesser charge for the greater good of all involved. They agreed. So, I subsequently asked Bruno to work with me and help us, the police, crack open this very serious case and to bring the suspects to justice. He agreed to work with me, and I gave him my personal cell phone number to contact me at any time. I hugged him and escorted him out of the police station. On his way out, I reminded Bruno that our deal could be revoked at any time he didn't hold up his end of the arrangement. I felt good about helping the kid, but even more so about the prospect of solving a significant case. Bruno stayed on as an informant for a while and I was able to get him his *green card.*

Chapter 9
Ocean's Eleven: Boston

Betrayal betrays the betrayer.

~ Erica Jong

So, now I'm still in uniform working this case. I began to dig into the information I had about Ocean's Eleven so much that I really couldn't effectively handle my uniformed assignment because the investigation was taking me all over Somerville and other nearby cities. I finally got permission from the Chief of Police to be temporarily reassigned to working the case in plain clothes. I was on a quest and was going to get these guys!

I went to see a guy named Tatiano, also known as *Mr. T;* I knew who was prominent in the Brazilian community in and around Sommerville. He had a stocky build and used to run with the gangs when he was younger. Tatiano seemed to know everything that was going on in town with the Brazilians. I asked him if he had heard anything about Ocean's Eleven and all of the break-ins targeting the affluent Brazilians in town. He said he'd heard a few things, but he couldn't provide me with any information I could use to build my case. Finally, Tatiano said, "Hey, man. Let me hook you up with this guy I know named Leon. If anyone knows anything about this stuff, it's him." Tatiano ended up arranging for Leon and me to meet at a Brazilian nightclub called the Samba Bar.

The drumbeat of Afro-Brazilian music could be heard from half a block away on this hot summer night. At the Samba Bar and Grill on Somerville Avenue, I nursed my club soda with lime at the bar as the band played. I probably would have had something a little stronger – but I was working. I wore cargo shorts and my signature loose-fitting Red Sox shirt to hide my gun, badge, and cuffs. Beautiful Brazilian girls danced and laughed on the dance floor while the guys watched and occasionally joined them. I sat off in the corner, waiting to see who was flashing wads of cash, or parking their new Corvettes, Range Rovers, and assorted German cars out front.

Somerville may have declared their status as a sanctuary city and refused to cooperate with federal immigration officials. However, there were still issues that went along with being undocumented – like not having a social security number. You need a social security number to open up a bank account, so without that, most business owners in the area did the next best thing. They installed safes in their homes and kept quiet about it. They did what generations of immigrants in this area before them did. They worked hard and saved their money in hopes of a better life for themselves and their families.

This American dream would have worked out well if it weren't for the crew going around stealing these people's life savings. This crew was hitting so many houses that neighboring police departments were getting regular complaints of busted safes abandoned on the side of public streets.

I was determined to round up every one of these assholes and shut this crew down.

While watching the high rollers, who were watching the women, I noticed one guy in jeans and a golf shirt across the room that couldn't keep his eyes off me. As I watched an older guy pay the bartender with a hundred-dollar bill, I realized that the guy in the golf shirt was now standing next to me, staring at me with a slight smile. I stared back. He was about 5' 7", lean and muscular, with short dark hair. The top two buttons of his shirt were unbuttoned, revealing a thick Cuban link chain and the top portion of an enormous dragon tattoo that covered his chest. I looked behind me to see if he was smiling at someone else. There was no one there. I looked back, and his smile was gone, but he was looking at me straight-dead in the eyes now. I leaned in close to him. "Can I help you with something?"

The question and my tone startled him, and his smart-ass smile returned as he laughed nervously. "You know, I have been watching you. You're a cop." He put his hands up; palms open in a submissive gesture. "No problem. I just always wanted to be a cop, but that's very difficult to do in Brazil." He put his hand out. 'My name is Leon."

I stood up and shook his hand. It was the hand of someone who works for a living – strong and stained black in spots where it won't come clean no matter how much scrubbing you do.

"My name is Mario. What do you do for a living, Leon?"

"I work at an auto body shop."

He took a seat next to me and began to tell me about his life and how he had overstayed his visa and needed to find a way to get a green card. He was living at his aunt's house in Brookline and had some problems with his girlfriend.

I listened and nodded as he poured out his life story. "I can't help you with your girlfriend situation, but I may be able to help you with your immigration status," I said.

One of the most enticing things an investigator can offer is an 'S Visa.' S Visas, or "snitch visas," as they are often called, are reserved for individuals who provide law enforcement agencies assistance. If a CI provides exceptional aid and has a relatively clean record, they can earn Legal Permanent Resident Status through their work.

I had Leon's attention now. The chance to play cop and maybe earn his green card was enticing to him. "I can help. So, are you a drug cop?"

I looked at him, trying to figure out if he was digging for information or actually trying to do some work for me. I took a sip of my drink and set it back on the bar.

"I'm looking for guns. Drugs are good too, but right now, I'm looking for the guys that are breaking into houses."

"That's easy. I know these guys."

But, I thought, he has to be bullshitting me. It can't be this easy. "Well, if you know them can you get me in with them?"

Leon made a face like he just bit a lemon. "No way, dude, they'd sniff you out just like I did. But I can get close to them. They're all Brazilian like me. I'm friends with *Scrappy*. When they rob a house, he takes all the passports they stole. He's the best. He cuts out the original picture and then puts someone else's picture over it. That's how people get driver's licenses."

I said, "Okay, if you know who is doing this, tell me one thing, how do they know which houses to break into?"

Leon looked around and then moved in closely to whisper in my ear. "Cleaning ladies. Their girlfriends are all cleaning ladies. They go through the fuckin' houses and take videos of safes, gold, checkbooks, everything. So they know when no one is home too." Leon giggled like a kid that was telling on his sister for skipping school.

I put my hands up to my face like I was praying, looked at the ceiling, and smiled. Finally, I got just the piece of information that I needed. Leon had just corroborated what Bruno had told me. Even if this guy doesn't deliver, I can probably track these guys down through the cleaners.

I gave him my card. "Let's talk soon, like tomorrow at the station."

On my way home to Billerica, I thought about the possibilities that were now on the table, having a source like this. A good Confidential Informant (CI) can do things and go places a cop can't. A good CI can spend days partying with bad guys, getting high, and sometimes even committing a few minor crimes along the way. All the while taking note of who did what. Some of these people do it for the money. Some do it to work off a beef or to settle a score. Some do it for a green card. But, in the end, they all want something.

So, once again, I'm having money problems. The department will only pay $40 per buy to a CI, and since Leon wasn't a criminal, he wasn't working off a beef, so until I could get him a green card, I could only pay him $40 for each undercover operation. So I needed to pass Leon to the Bureau of Alcohol Tobacco Firearms and Explosives (ATF) if I wanted to keep him going. They had the money, the resources, and the ability to have his immigration status adjusted.

The very next day, Leon came to the PD. We went up to the detective's office and picked up where we left off. "Mario, these guys are serious people. One of them is my friend. They drive the nicest cars around. They have their hands in everything. They break into cars; they break into houses. They hang around at a club in Revere. It's called Wonderland." The information was general, kind of what I had already gathered from the patterns and other sources. But I needed specifics!

"Leon, I need names and locations. What do you have?"

He hesitated for a second. "I know that they robbed a house yesterday and took a safe," he said.

"Where?"

Leon said, "I don't know the exact address, but it's a big yellow house near Main Street in Malden."

"Perfect. That's what I need. Give me a call if you get any more info, but don't push it. I don't want them to get suspicious?"

As soon as he left, I called Malden PD and was transferred to Detective Trent Headley. "Did you guys have a break-in at a yellow house on Main Street yesterday?"

Detective Trent Headley looked through the log and said, "Yup - sure did. How do you know?"

"I have a CI; I think I might know the names of the people that did it. I'm working on it now. I'll get it."

So now, I'm validating the information that Leon brought me. It's all checking out. He's really in with these guys, and this kid is no joke. He calls me every couple of days with information about break-ins. Each time I'd call the local PDs – Malden, Medford, Everett, Charlestown, they would go to the address and find a kicked-in door or a broken window. We miss these guys by a minute or two each time, but now we have their street names. The deeper Leon gets, the more we start piecing this together.

Chapter 10
Strike While the Iron is Hot!

*Pursue one great decisive aim with
force and determination.*

~ Carl von Clausewitz

I was relentless in my pursuit of the Ocean's Eleven crew. I had already identified several members of the band of thieves and arrested them. I loved doing this kind of work – detective work! My chief noticed how much I enjoyed it too. I was promoted to detective in 2005 and assigned as an investigator in the Property Crimes Unit. Now I can finish what I started with these Brazilian bandits.

One day, I was working on an unrelated case with Sergeant Brooks from the Massachusetts State Police, at their station, off McGrath Highway. We were just about to head out to lunch at White Sports Subs on Medford Avenue when I got a text from Leon.

"Dude, Nanga is hitting a house today."

"Where?"

"Everett. Shute Street"

"That's the dude with the blue Mustang with the fin, right?"

"That's him, but someone dropped him off."

Sergeant Brooks and I jumped in his black Ford Fusion and took off for Everett. While en-route, I called Everett PD and told them to meet me in

80

Glendale Square, near American Nutrition Center. Everett is an industrial city, very blue-collar. Everett has always been a city of immigrants; at one time, Everett was all Irish and Italian. Today, Everett is a mix of Brazilian, Haitian, Guatemalan, and holdouts from generations past.

The city is filled with multi-family homes on tree-lined streets. Everett is an excellent option for rental properties for new arrivals to the Boston area with public transportation to neighboring Boston. Unfortunately, it is also a perfect recipe for overcrowding and crime. As new immigrants settle en masse over the years, the second and third generations of immigrants from Europe head further north into the suburbs. The storefronts that sold cold cuts and subs, like Luigi's and Angelina's, have all been replaced by Brazilian markets, cafes, and beauty salons. That's how it is, at least until the next generation of immigrants moves to the city and forces the Brazilians out. It's been this way in the Greater Boston Area since the Mayflower landed 41 miles away at Plymouth Rock.

I saw the two unmarked cars waiting for us at the bottom of Broadway. They followed us to Shute Street. As we crept down the street, I counted the house numbers up when I saw movement out of the corner of my eye. It was Nanga. He had already robbed the house and walked down the driveway, hands in pocket, head turning side to side, looking ever so arrogant and satisfied with himself. He spotted us and stopped dead in his tracks. He started to back pedal. I opened the passenger door, and he turned around and took off like a shot. It was on.

I sprinted after him, he was young, fast, and wiry, but I was determined. As I ran through the driveway, I ran past the door he had kicked in. With each fence we went over, I closed more distance on him. My heart was pounding, and my throat was so dry I could hardly speak. Dropping down from the third fence, he lost his footing and tried to recover, but it was too late. I was on him. I clothes-lined him to the ground. He struggled while I got the first cuff on. I twisted the cuff, putting pressure on his wrist until he gave me his other arm. He was done. As I pulled him to his feet, he stood defiantly. After booking him at Everett Station, I pulled him into an interview. I told him I knew about his whole crew, and he was going to give me their names. He shook his head, jutted his chin out, and said, "I ain't telling you shit." True to his word, he gave up no one and did his time.

Over the next few months, we hit the crew hard. We had six of the eleven serving time on various charges: armed robbery, document fraud, and breaking and entering. The list went on. We had systematically taken out the leadership of the crew. However, even with them locked away, they still had contact with the outside world and were still calling shots outside of their prison walls.

Yes, 2005 was a good year! I was solving cases, and my wife Christy was already pregnant with our first child. The two of us were settled into our Billerica home. A sleepy little town north of Boston.

Billerica was a breath of fresh air for most people to escape the city, in fact, so much so that many people called Billerica Somerville with trees. But make no mistake, they are two very different towns.

After finishing my shift at midnight, I got home and climbed into bed. I was exhausted and fell right into a deep sleep. At 3:00 am, I could hear my cell phone downstairs ringing. I walked down and saw that I missed three back-to-back calls from Leon. Standing in my kitchen, with no lights on, I dialed him back – he answered on the first ring.

"Don't fuckin' talk, just listen, get out of the house, right now."

"What are you talking about."

"Get your wife and get the fuck out now! They're on their way to Billerica, to your house. They're going to kill you and your wife and burn the house down."

I ran back upstairs and got my gun. I told my wife to stay in the bedroom. It was the safest place for her. I called my brother, John, and said, get up here now and bring plenty of firepower. It was too dangerous to leave the house now. What if they had someone set up watching. I checked all the locks and waited for my brother. John showed up minutes later, loaded for bear. I stood watch out the front, and my brother watched the back. At 6:00 am, I called the chief of detectives and told him the deal. He said, standby, I got you covered. Thirty minutes later, a convoy of cruisers and a Bearcat containing an entire SWAT Team came speeding up to my house with snipers and assaulter.

They set up a perimeter around the house. Most of my neighbors didn't know what I did for work at this point. They knew now. I felt bad. I moved here to get away from this shit, and now all this craziness was here. We snuck my wife out with a protective detail, and she went to stay with her parents. I spent the next three days at the house.

Half the SWAT Team would be on duty around the house, and the other half would take breaks in my living room. They would ask me questions about the case. I ordered pizzas and cokes for them three times a day, making sure I fed every shift. On one of those such evenings, the pizza delivery guy came walking up to the front of my house. It was dark outside, and the law enforcement personnel assigned around my house could not see what the young man was carrying in his hands. So they conducted a full tactical assault on the poor pizza delivery kid. They rushed him, pointing guns and yelling commands for him to get down on the ground. He didn't know what hit him. It all happened so fast – he crapped himself! After picking him up and dusting him off, I apologized profusely and shook his hand. In the end, I left him a really big tip for his troubles.

After three days, I was more determined ever to finish this case. They threatened my family. They wanted to kill my pregnant wife and burn down my house! Fortunately, that never came to fruition, and we eventually were able to resume somewhat of a normal life.

Chapter 11
The Self-servant

Mercenaries and auxiliaries are useless and dangerous; and if one holds his state based on these arms, he will stand neither firm nor safe; for they are disunited, ambitious, and without discipline, unfaithful, valiant before friends, cowardly before enemies; they have neither the fear of God nor fidelity to men, and destruction is deferred only so long as the attack is; for in peace, one is robbed by them, and in war by the enemy.

~ Niccolò Machiavelli

Sources and CIs, by nature, are not to be trusted. They are an evil – a necessary evil. We pay them to betray their own. They are freelancers, mercenaries in the world of intelligence. They stand for no cause other than self-preservation and personal gain. They don't do it for their country, and they don't do it for the flag. Their allegiance is to themselves. They live in both worlds and play both sides against the middle. The integrity of a CI's word is constantly being weighed and tested. We spend half of our time watching the bad guys and the other half watching our CIs. It's a dangerous game because we rely on our CIs to introduce us to criminal networks. One screw up, and we're dead. That is also how we become close with them. We share crazy experiences and share in the danger. It's a deal with the devil.

If things go wrong on a buy, our backup is all of the way down the road. They'll probably do an excellent job of drawing a chalk line around my body by the time they get here. But my CI is right in the belly of the beast with me, and who better? After all, he's no stranger to violence and treachery. When we're buying guns from a criminal high on PCP, our CI shares that danger with us; it's like having a Pitbull that's been trained to bite; you know he might be a danger to the mailman, but you let it go because he thinks he's protecting you. That is until he turns around and bites your hand.

A week before we grabbed Nanga, we got a call from Citizens Bank. There was a customer there, and he was cashing a check. Only the checks had been previously reported stolen. Special Agent Campbell and I rolled up to the bank, and wouldn't you know it, it was Jeffrey, Ocean's Eleven's fraudulent document maker. He had been on my radar for a while, and now we had him red-handed. We introduced ourselves, and immediately his shoulders slumped, and we cuffed him. We brought him back to the station. I knew he was going to flip. He wasn't a gangster-like Nanga; he was deeper, always ready to make a deal. I didn't let on that I knew he was in with the crew. I just told him there were a bunch of break-ins, and he could either go to jail now or help himself by working this off. He said he would help and thanked me profusely. I called him the next day.

"Jeffrey, It's Mario; what do you have for me?"

He said he had something big—a human smuggler in Everett. He said the guy had been threatening to kill him. "He's here illegally and sells fake documents." This information wouldn't help me with Ocean's Eleven but would be a good arrest for the guys at ICE. I called my contact at ICE and gave him the information. He said they would go by the house at 5:30 pm. I finished up some paperwork at the station and headed over to the house to link up with ICE for the arrest. I called ICE when I arrived and found out they had already arrested him. I decided to stick around for a few minutes to see if anyone else came or went from the house. I had a sinking suspicion that something wasn't right. Not five minutes later, who do I see? Stupid Jeffrey, walking out the door of the home with a small safe in his hands. He looked like the cat that swallowed the canary. I could feel my blood pressure going through the roof. I squeezed the steering wheel as hard as possible and kicked the door open. I could feel the veins in my neck bulging as I swore at him through clenched teeth.

"You dirty bastard! You got that guy deported so you could rob him."

"He's a piece of shit. He tried to screw me over. This is the money he owed me."

Every bit the opportunist, Jeffrey saw his cooperation as an opportunity to get rid of the competition. His code wouldn't let him rat on his friends, but there was enough moral flexibility within that code to sell out his competition. This behavior is essentially a *Code of Ethics* with these guys. But as the saying goes, there are no swans in the gutter. Ordinary people can't do this work; bad guys would sense that they were different. This was my mistake. At the end of the day, ICE took a bad guy off the street. But the lesson stayed with me. The CI world is dirty - dirty but necessary.

One by one, we took down the rest of Ocean's Eleven. We got Paulo trying to cash forged checks at a bank. We pinched Francisco in the process of breaking into a house. Carlos got arrested for hitting his girlfriend. I had a separate warrant waiting for him right after his booking. We put them all in jail, and afterward, ICE had detainers waiting for them, and they all got deported back to Brazil. I was ecstatic. I dedicated over a year of my life to get these guys. It was all made possible by Leon.

Front page of *Somerville Journal*, 2005

Chapter 12
The Good Detective

Every man, at the bottom of his heart,
believes that he is a born detective.

~ John Buchan

One sleepy Sunday morning in 2006, I was in my unmarked detective car cruising down Interstate 93 into Somerville from Billerica when I heard the alert tone over my radio about an armed robbery in progress in the city. We don't usually get calls like that at 7:00 am on a Sunday. I thought to myself, *what is even open this early on a Sunday?* Just then, the dispatcher comes over the radio, "Control, Delta-6." I answered, "Delta-6, go ahead." "Delta-6, respond to the 100 block of Broadway for an armed robbery and sexual assault that had just occurred." I was still a way out from the city, so I lit up the blue lights and jammed down the highway. *Here we go – there's no rest for the weary.*

The victim was just being carted off in an ambulance as I arrived on scene. The crime scene was inside a laundromat. One of the patrol officers told me the victim was a 23-year-old Brazilian female who had just been robbed at gunpoint and viciously raped. So, I went inside the laundromat and did my *detective thing,* searching for physical evidence of the crime and digital evidence like surveillance camera footage. But there wasn't anything available. So, I conducted a canvass for witnesses, and there were none. I was a bit frustrated because I was batting zero so far. So, I decided to go to the hospital to talk to my victim.

I contacted the victim, Adriana, who was visibly shaken by the ordeal she had just gone through. She told me she is an employee at the laundromat who provides wash and fold service for their customers. In other words, if you had a bundle of laundry to do, you'd drop it off in the morning, and Adriana would wash, dry, and fold it for you. It would be all folded and ready for you to pick up when you returned later in the day.

Adriana stated that one of her regular customers, a gentleman, had come into the laundromat and dropped off his laundry to be picked up later in the afternoon. She wrote him a receipt and put her copy in the receipt bin. Just as her customer walked out of the business, the suspect entered the building. The suspect got behind Adriana and put a gun to her head. He put his free hand down the front of her pants and told her he'd kill her if she didn't do what he told her to do.

The suspect dragged Adriana behind the cash register and demanded that she open it up. After she complied with his demands, he put the money in his pockets, pushed her down onto the ground behind the counter, and proceeded to rape her. After he was finished, he got his baggy pants pulled up, and he slowly walked out the front door of the business as if nothing had happened at all. Adriana said the suspect's gun was a black pistol with scratches on it. It had a *"long thing sticking out from the bottom of the handle"* (extended magazine). I got a description of the suspect from her, concluded my interview, and left the hospital.

I decided to go back to the laundromat to locate the receipt she told me about that she had placed in the receipt bin. I looked in the container, and sure enough, there it was – the receipt with the customer's name and phone number. Bingo! I called the number and spoke with the customer, who remembered seeing a young black male hanging out next to a parking meter in front of the laundromat as he left. "Did you get a good look at him," I asked? "Yes, sir, I did." *This is great,* I thought. "Would you be able to identify him if you saw him again?" He replied, "I'm pretty sure I could." I asked him to come to our station to work with a sketch artist in producing a composite sketch of the suspect's face.

I called Jack Skinner from Concord Police Department, a neighboring jurisdiction located northwest of Somerville. He is an experienced sketch artist that some of the other local agencies use on their cases because they don't have a sketch artist of their own. The witness and Jack worked together to produce a very accurate and true-to-life-looking composite of our suspect. Meanwhile, this incident made it all over the news because it was such a heinous crime. Our mayor and police chief were both quoted as saying, "We will find and bring the perpetrator to justice."

I disseminated the sketch around my department, asking if anyone had had contact with anybody that resembled the person in the drawing. One of the officers told me, "That looks like Rashad Campbell." I told him, "No way. Campbell is 15 years old. What kind of 15-year-old kid robs and violently rapes someone on a Sunday morning?" Ironically, in a twist of fate, my brother John was working patrol on the following Sunday morning. I received a call from him, and he told me he saw Rashad walking down the street and had detained him. He asked me if I had enough evidence to arrest him, but I informed him that I didn't know at that point. I asked John to take a picture of Rashad and send it to me, which he subsequently did. When I compared the image to the sketch, it was definitely the same guy, right down to the oversized, fake diamond stud earring in his right ear.

As I continued following leads on the case, I got called into work by a patrol sergeant on the following weekend. It turns out his officers got called to the local K-mart store at the mall regarding a shoplifter that the store's loss prevention people were holding. They caught a kid stealing merchandise in the store. When they went to detain him, the kid resisted, and a scuffle ensued. A black pistol fell out of the suspect's waistband onto the floor during the altercation. The gun had scratches on it and an extended magazine. You guessed it – the thief was

Rashad Campbell. While the patrol guys dealt with Rashad and the loss prevention folks, I was busy getting a search warrant to retrieve Rashad's DNA.

Some folks may find it hard to believe, but Rashad was released into the custody of his mother. So, the next day I went over to Rashad's house to interview the kid and get his DNA. I was told Rashad was at a laundromat with his mother – go figure! I went over to the laundromat and found them there. I told the mother that I had evidence her son had committed the rape that was all over the TV news. I told her I had a warrant to retrieve Rashad's DNA, and she wanted nothing to do with it. She started getting belligerent with me and said her son would never do such a horrific thing as raping a woman. Just as she was about to try to leave the laundromat, Rashad grabbed his mother's arm and said, "Mom, I did it." There it is in simple terms that everyone can understand.

I interviewed Rashad, obtained his DNA, and put this case to bed once and for all. However, even though we solve crimes, the issue isn't over for everyone. Many victims still suffer even after the fact. Sometimes I still think about Adriana to this day, wondering how or if she was able to move past the trauma of being violently attacked, raped, and robbed. I pray that she lives a peaceful life and has been healed from her emotional scars.

Chapter 13
A Star Is Born

Stardom isn't a profession; it's an accident.

~ Lauren Bacall

I wanted to focus Leon on getting guns off the street. Yes, I still kept him working as a CI, even after Ocean's Eleven was behind us. We needed him to start getting the word out that he was someone who could move firearms. He had spent a lot of time by now with different members of the now-imprisoned crew and had established himself as someone that could run in those circles. It was time for Leon to make his foray into the world of gun smugglers. I told him to start putting the word out that he wanted to buy guns. He got busy with his new assignment, started asking around, flashing cash, and just like moths to a flame, gun runners began finding him.

"That guy from Woburn called; he has the burners." It was Leon calling; he was itching to get these guns. I walked away from my wife in the living room. If I had a nickel for every time I had to walk away from my family to take one of these calls, I'd be a millionaire. "Alright, slow down. How many guns does he have?" Leon took a breath. "Two guns. At least, maybe more. He wants $2,700 for them."

Now, I'm a local detective; we don't have that kind of money laying around. We do low-level stuff, $200 cocaine buys, maybe some OxyContin—that kind of thing. But I want these guns off the street. I'm in a jam here. We have Leon running around like a high roller, telling these guys that he runs guns, and now we don't even have enough money to buy two guns. Leon was waiting for me to make a decision and talking a mile a minute. "You know what, Leon, set it up for tomorrow. We'll take them.

I had to get creative and fast. So the following day, I called the ATF.

Danny answered: "ATF."

"Danny, this is detective Mario Oliveira from Somerville. I have a CI that set up a gun buy today, and we don't have the money. We need $2,700."

Danny paused, taking in what I was telling him. "I'll be right there. I'll get the money.

From my desk, I saw Danny in the doorway of the detective's office. He was in his forties and stood about 6'1" with blondish brown hair. I was on the desk phone, so I waved him over. He wore a button-down shirt, untucked with jeans. His bow-legged walk and the way he moved told me he was an athlete, a hockey player, to be exact.

We met with Leon in a nearby parking lot, and I introduced Danny. I took Leon's hat off and had him turn around while I searched him; he looked surprised but was okay with it. Next, Danny activated the hidden recorders. Searching a source was a standard operating procedure. We did it in case a defense lawyer accused our source of bringing the guns to the deal himself.

As Leon slipped into the dark leather driver's seat of the undercover BMW X5, he looked like a little kid getting into his dad's car with his learner's permit. "You guys roll around in this shit." The black-on-black SUV was wired inside and out for video and sound. The vehicle definitely looked like the car of a high-level gun runner, but I worried about Leon pulling it off. He looked the part with his gold chain and flat-brimmed hat. But it would take more than clothes; he needed the demeanor.

As he sat wide-eyed in the BMW, I knew I had to get his head back in the game. "Hey buddy, remember what we talked about. This guy is not screwing around; don't be laughing and shit. This is business - I want you to get these guns and push him for more. See if you can get ten." He put on his serious face and got right into the role. He could turn it on and off like a light switch. One minute, he was fooling around; the next minute, he was like, you better have these guns, or we're going to have a problem!

As we rolled out of the backlot, Danny in his Explorer and me in my Ford Taurus, we were careful not to get too close. I could see the BMW's tail lights in the distance up ahead. It was like sending your kid to school for the first time in many ways. First, you're responsible for him, and now he's taking a risk for you. Thoughts went through my head of everything that could possibly go wrong. However, I had one benefit going for me; I would be able to understand what they were saying. The car was wired up for real-time sound, and even though the Brazilian dialect was slightly different, I was used to it, and I speak Portuguese, just like them.

As Leon parked, I saw Adilson walk up (dark-skinned, jeans, and hoodie) and hop in the passenger side of the X5. Then, they got right to business. As soon as the door shut, I could hear Leon over the wire say, "Yo, show me the shit."

Adilson pulled out two Glocks from his waistband. One .40 caliber and one 9mm. Leon began counting the money out loud, one hundred at a time. I looked at Danny.

"He's got the guns."

After he paid Adilson, Leon asked, "Can you get any more?"

"Yeah, I can get more."

"Where you gettin' this shit from?"

"The Carolinas. I drive down to fuckin' North Carolina. I can get you all you can handle."

"Good. I need ten more."

"I'll be in touch."

We waited for Adilson to leave, and I texted Leon to take a left out of the parking lot, drive two blocks, do a U-turn, and keep driving straight. We ran a surveillance detection route (SDR), ensuring no one was following Leon. We met him in a triple-decker parking lot, and Danny took possession of the two guns. I could tell he was happy. This was a good buy, and we were set up now for a much bigger purchase. We were working our way up the chain to see where these guns were coming in from. Danny started running the serial numbers through ETrace. ETrace tells the history of a firearm - where it was built, what shop it went to, and its last owner before ending up on the black market.

The next day, I'm writing reports about the buy, and my phone rings, it's Leon.

"The fucking guy called me already. He's going to get more guns."

"When?"

"Tomorrow, he's flying to North Carolina and renting a car. Then, he said he'll meet me in Woburn and sell me the guns when he returns."

The following day, Danny and I drove up to Woburn and set up surveillance on Adilson's house. Adislon lived right across the street from an elementary school, so we watched from the parking lot. He walked out his front door a short time later and jumped in a sports car. He was driving like a maniac through neighborhoods. We struggled to maintain distance and not lose him, so we got close behind him, what we call *bumper lock*. As we sped down I93 south, weaving in and out of lanes, I thought about how reckless this guy was. I also thought about how sloppy he was, speeding and weaving through traffic. Finally, as I watched the cars we were passing go by in a blur, I thought about how big this was.

This wasn't small-time buys anymore; this was ten handguns. The same guns that are ending up on the streets of Boston. Each one of these guns would end up taking a life, maybe two. Just then, I felt myself lurch forward as the seat belt yanked me back into my seat; I instinctively braced my feet on the floor as Danny jammed on the breaks and came to a stop in the now grid-locked 93 traffic. I looked at Danny and said, "This guy's a maniac."

As we got close to Logan International Airport, I searched Google to figure out what airline he was traveling on. Tonight, the only airline going to Charlotte is American Airlines; Terminal B. Adislon pulled into Airport Central Parking, and Danny dropped me off at Terminal B's departure level. I found a chokepoint to start my surveillance. There was only one way into the terminal from Central Parking. So, I positioned myself between that corridor and the ticket counter.

I waited nervously; as the minutes ticked away, I wondered if he was on a different airline or knew surveillance was onto him, so he pulled into a garage. Savvy bad guys with counter-surveillance experience often pull into garages if they think they're being followed, especially by aircraft. Then I see him coming down the escalator. He's the only person without a bag in the terminal. The Massachusetts State Police are the public safety agency for Logan International Airport. I contact my friend, State Trooper Sgt. Steve Lopes, who happened to be working at the airport that day. He provided assistance with getting me into the airport's secure areas to conduct my surveillance.

As Adilson walked into the roped-off area of the ticket counter, I got in line behind him. I pulled out my phone and pretended to be texting while I shot video of him. He handed the ticket agent his license. I heard her say, "Charlotte, gate B18, boarding time is 6:30." I followed Adilson to the security line and watched as he went through. When I got back to the car, I looked at Danny. "Yup, he's heading to Charlotte."

The next night, Danny came to the station. We were going back and forth with the US Attorney's Office. We spent hours writing affidavits, search warrants, arrest warrants, and arrest operation plans. Finally, we had all of our ducks in a row and would be taking a lot of guns off the street, along with a real dangerous dude. I was typing away and could hear Danny speaking on his phone. "You gotta be fucking kidding me," he said. "Alright, it is what it is."

Danny hung up and shook his head. "That moron just got arrested, speeding up I95, in North Carolina."

Danny's shoulders slumped forward, and he stared at the floor. "He blew past a three-person interdiction team from North Carolina State Police. They yanked him over and asked him where he was coming from, and he said vacation in Florida. The only problem was he had no luggage. Speeding, out-of-state plates, and his horseshit vacation stories must've set their bullshit meter off. They put the heat on him and told them they would search the car. He copped to having the Guns. They called ATF down there, and they found ten firearms secreted all over his car. They got the arrest."

I couldn't believe it. This bust would've been a massive seizure. But, it wasn't a total loss; our work leading up to the arrest was a big part of the case. We were also answering a very big question; where are the guns coming from - North Carolina.

In fact, things were going so well; that Danny told me that they had a slot for me as a Task Force Officer at the ATF. Federal Agencies, like the Bureau of Alcohol, Tobacco, Firearms, and Explosives (ATF), DEA, and FBI, often bring on local detectives and feds from other agencies into their agencies as Task Force Officers (TFO). The local cops called all of the federal law enforcement entities *"alphabet soup agencies"* because they were never referred to by their full name but rather by their three-letter acronyms. TFOs essentially take on the duties of their host agencies while bringing specialties and necessary experience. The TFOs get federally deputized and perform the same functions as their host agency. So, I would be bringing my street experience and one of the best sources in the business.

I was in a good spot. My chief, Mike Cabral, signed off on the deal, and I was reassigned to an ATF Task Force located out of the Boston Field Office, Group 6. The task force's purpose was simple – to get illegal guns off the street and go after illicit gunrunners. Unfortunately, it was a lucrative business for the gunrunners who purchased firearms unlawfully, sold illegally, and ended up in the hands of criminal street gangs.

Things were also going well for Leon. He was like a little brother to me. I never viewed him as a criminal because he wasn't; he just wanted a green card. So, we got that for him, and we also paid him well for his work. He was finally where he wanted to be; he had moved off his aunt's couch and into an apartment with the love of his life, Paulina.

Chapter 14
Belo Horizonte

*They don't have to tell me what
life is like in a ghetto.*

~ George Blanda

Hildo DeCunha came to Everett, Massachu-setts, in 2001, by way of Belo Horizonte, home to the most dangerous favela (slum) in Brazil. With a homicide rate of 29.74 per 100,000 residents, freelance killing is big business, and human life is very cheap. In fact, in 2015, more civilians were killed in Brazil than in Syria during the peak of ISIS and a civil war.

While his compatriots set up shop in the new land, Hildo set up his own shop near Everett Square in a single-family house that was converted into a secret multi-family dwelling with padlocks on bedroom doors and a shared bathroom. While his housemates got up in the morning to hang sheetrock, clean houses, and work their day jobs, Hildo also went to work plying the only trade he knew, running guns from down south to Massachusetts, and weighing out mounds of powder cocaine on digital triple beam scales. So naturally, he bagged it up into half grams, grams, and eight balls for sale to the locals. Hildo was a wolf in sheep's clothing. Most Brazilians moved here to get away from crime and violence. Hildo brought with him everything they were fleeing from. He was a former contract killer who had one thing on his mind – making as much money as possible and going back to Brazil to live out his days and never work again unless the price was right.

Leon managed to get linked up with Hildo, who had his fingers in almost every criminal enterprise imaginable; guns, drugs, girls – trafficking and selling them all. Leon eventually started going on *gun runs* with Hildo down to North Carolina. Hildo was the key because he had already established a relationship with a more significant gun dealer.

I told Leon that I wanted to get to the *bigger fish,* and we would use Hildo to do it. Hildo told Leon he needed to get his hands on fifteen more guns and said he would score them from his North Carolina connection. He would arrange a meet and swap – guns for cash, and Leon would accompany him. Leon and Hildo got in a vehicle, went off, and did the deal. We ran surveillance on them the whole time. When Leon dropped off Hildo at his house, Hildo hid the guns in some five-gallon containers.

I met up with Leon after he left Hildo's house. Leon gave me all of the details I needed to hit the home and recover the illicit firearms. Because we knew Hildo was slinging drugs out of his apartment, we already had a search warrant for drugs in hand. In addition, the SWAT team was already set up near the house. So, I gave them the signal to move in. It seemed to me like SWAT cops were going in through doors, windows, and just about anywhere they could gain entry into the house. They moved hard and fast!

After SWAT secured the premises, some other investigators and I began a systematic search of the property. Of course, we found the guns as expected, along with drugs, cash, and other stolen goods. We hit the jackpot. It was a good day for law enforcement and the community.

We continued to work on this case which led us to the more significant link in the criminal enterprise chain of knuckleheads – Hildo's connection in North Carolina. I told Leon I wanted to get to the guy in North Carolina and asked him if he could broker a meeting with us. Leon said he probably could do it, and he had the perfect story to make it happen.

Leon called "Tito" in North Carolina and told him that Hildo got busted for dealing drugs out of his house. Tito said, "Man, I told that fool not to be slinging that shit out of his pad. It ain't good for what we all got going on!" Leon said, "Yeah, man. Hildo is all dried up, and I can't count on him to get guns anymore, with him being in jail and all. I want you to meet a guy who needs to get his hands on some guns. He's solid and legit, man." So, Tito and Leon planned a meeting between the three of us. I was posing as a gang banger from Boston that needed more guns so we could start doing drive-byes on rival gang members in the area.

Leon and I met up with Tito in Fayetteville and talked. Leon put on his scary guy face and did the introduction. Of course, I was in my trademark baggy Boston Red Sox jersey and wearing a wire. I told Tito I needed pistols, Uzis, and fully-automatic rifles if he could swing it. Tito said it was possible to make it happen, but he would need some time to get all of the guns. Leon and I parted ways with Tito, and I was pumped that the first part of the plan came together so well as we left Tito's apartment building.

Finally, the day came when Leon got the call from Tito about having the guns in his possession. We set up another meeting so I could do the transaction with him. But this time, I would not only be wired up but would have the full support of a SWAT team, aviation units, and cops in marked squad cars at the ready. In addition, I had the *bait money* with me to pay Tito with. The bait money would later be used as evidence if the case went to trial. We had already taken pictures of the money. We recorded the serial numbers so that we could accurately testify those were the exact identical one-hundred-dollar bills that were in the defendant's possession at the time of his subsequent arrest.

Leon went on the operation with me. Tito's instructions were to meet him in the back of the apartment complex, and we would do the deal there. It was in broad daylight, and when I asked him about people seeing us and drawing attention to ourselves, he said, "Nah, it's just a bunch of old people living around here. They won't notice anything." I was driving a non-descript rental car that I had rented at the airport in Charlotte. I pulled around to the back of the complex, looking for Tito. But we had beat Tito to the location and waited around for him to arrive. The thought did cross my mind, *what if he tries to burn me, and this is just a setup for him to rip me off?* However, there were a couple of work vans with an entire SWAT team hiding in the back. There were even one or two guys dressed as cable TV repairmen who just blended into the scenery.

I was wearing a ball cap. The predetermined signal was for me to remove my hat when the deal was done, at which time the SWAT team would move in and do the takedown. There was even a SWAT sniper on a nearby rooftop who was watching us. If things went wrong, I was to hit the ground, and the sniper would take out Tito and any other bad guys from his rooftop position. There were also uniformed police officers located nearby but out of public view.

Tito finally drove into the parking lot in a pickup truck with a bed cover. He pulled the bed of his truck up to the trunk of my rental car. After a brief discussion, he lifted the lid on the truck's bed, revealing a massive cache of weapons. I gave Tito the money, and I took off my ball cap to scratch my head. As I took my hat off, the entire parking lot was swarming with cops. Tito didn't know what had hit him, and I believe he was in shock.

Our next part of the trip took a bizarre turn. Leon and I met up with John, one of the ATF agents who was part of the team at the Charlotte Douglas International Airport. Because John and I were flying armed, we had to get checked in by the airport police and show them our law enforcement credentials. John, Leon, and I walked to the gate to catch our flight that was supposed to leave in about 30 minutes. Leon decided to use the men's room before boarding the flight as we were waiting in line. John also followed Leon into the restroom. Within seconds, John came out of the men's room and started yelling, "Mario, Mario, get in here!"

I ran into the bathroom, at which time John pointed to one of the stalls where there was a guy down on the floor. I banged on the door and got no response. I went into the stall next to the man's stall and peered over the barrier. The unconscious man had apparently done his business by looking at the remnant he had left behind in the toilet. He was gurgling and doing what we in the first-responder world call the *death rattle*.

I kicked in the bathroom stall door and had John help drag the guy out. I said, "John, this guy is going to die. We need to do CPR." So, we took turns doing rescue breathing and chest compressions. Leon summoned the airport police, who attempted to revive the man with an automated external defibrillator (AED) to no avail, and the man was subsequently pronounced dead at the scene. John, Leon, and I gave our information to the airport police for their report and ran to the gate to board our flight. The plane almost left without us, but we made it.

There was still a lot of paperwork left to do and many weapons to book as evidence. It turned out to be an incredibly long day, but it was all worth the effort.

Chapter 15
Crash and Burn

Some rise by sin, and some by virtue fall.

~ William Shakespeare

We celebrated our success at a Bruins game. Danny's friend worked at the Fleet Center and brought us into a luxury box. It was just Danny, his neighbor, and me. Free food, free booze, and a perfect view of the action. The night couldn't have been better. Danny was talking about how great Leon did. Just then, I felt my phone buzzing in my pocket. It was Leon.

"Leon, your ears must be ringing; we were just talking about you."

I couldn't hear him, so I stepped out into the hallway. He was sobbing, and I couldn't understand him.

"What's wrong?'

"Pauli threw me out... and I robbed a bank. Everything is fucked up."

"What? Did you use a gun?"

"Yeah. I threw it in the Charles River."

I tried to talk him off the ledge, but he wasn't having any of it. So finally, I told him to turn himself in at Somerville PD, and I'd come right down. Realistically there was nothing I could do for him. This crime wasn't a simple drunk driving incident or a fight - he just robbed a damned bank. He kept apologizing. I could barely understand him through his sobbing. One thing was clear, though; he had his mind made up.

"I'm gonna undo what I did.'"

"How?"

"I'm gonna back out the way I snuck in – through Mexico."

"No, brother. Turn yourself in."

"I can't. These guys are suspicious of me. They'll kill me in there. The only place I am safe is in Brazil. I'm so sorry, Mario. I don't know what the fuck I'm doing."

That was it. He hung up and wouldn't answer my calls anymore. He threw his phone away. I worried about him. Worried he would get shot trying to flee. He would call me every couple of days from a burner phone or payphone. He would say, I just have to get across the border, and I'll be okay. I pleaded with him to turn himself in and said I would talk to the Assistant US Attorney for him. What was I going to say, though? He robbed a bank.

I couldn't sleep for days. The thoughts going through my head wouldn't allow me to. *What if he gets shot by police? Or what if he gets caught and they put him in prison, and he gets killed by Ocean's Eleven?* There were now wanted posters for him all over the United States.

One week later, as Leon was changing buses in El Paso, Texas, he was arrested by the US Marshals Fugitive Task Force. They extradited him back to Massachusetts. He was sentenced to three and a half years in state prison for the bank robbery, and just like the others he helped put away, ICE would be waiting for him too.

I sometimes wonder what would have happened if he had just called me instead of going into that bank. I can't comprehend how a break-up led to this, but it's not for me to judge. It's too bad that happened. But I held true to my word and got him his S-visa, or *snitch green card*. When I took him under my wing as a CI, I took responsibility for him, and it went bad.

Chapter 16
Hard Work Pays Off

The reward for work well done is the opportunity to do more.

~ Jonas Salk

As I began to settle into my new position, I continued to pound the pavement, working cases and developing new CIs. The work was meaningful to me, and I felt like I was making a difference – even in some small way. As I got some good experience in my task force job, the ATF created the Cross Border Initiative. The initiative's mission was to combat the flow of illegal firearms coming into Massachusetts from neighboring New England States. So, we began focusing our efforts on interstate gun trafficking.

The powers that be felt I was proficient and skilled enough as a TFO to start training people. My new trainee and partner, Brian Hudson, came to me straight out of the Federal Law Enforcement Training Center (FLETC) in Glynco, Georgia. But wait a minute! This guy is a brand-new ATF federal agent, and I'm just a local cop assigned to the task force. So how could it come to be that I was now responsible for training a new fed? I questioned it for a brief moment. But I came to realize that was just what ended up happening.

Brian was in his 40s. He was a former Army medic and served several combat tours in the middle-east.

The Cambridge Fire Department hired him after he got out of the Army. He decided to leave the fire service for his own reasons and become a cop. So, he got hired by the ATF. Brian was extremely intelligent but a little rough around the edges. I suppose being in the middle of the mix in Iran and Afghanistan during a time of war would do that to a person. He was also a very hard charger and eager to learn. At times, he was like an attack dog, and I felt I had to keep him on a tight leash.

Like any intelligent person with good common sense and sound judgment, Brian learned the job, the layout of the land, and how to follow investigative leads. As with any partner-to-partner relationship, patrol cop or detective, Brian and I bonded and got to know each other. How could we not? When you're with someone longer than you are with your own family every day, you tend to get to know that person quite well. We began to read each other's body language and picked up on each other's verbal cues. Sometimes I would know what Brian would do before reacting to something. That's just the way it is with partners. It's almost like a marriage except for the physical intimacy part.

One day in the summer of 2010, Brian was looking in the database we used to track firearms sales. All licensed gun dealers must report gun sales which are entered and logged into the electronic database. Brian called out to me, "Mario, come take a look at this." I walked over to Brian's desk as he pointed to his computer monitor. "Look at this. Talk about a red flag – ten gun purchases from different dealers in New Hampshire in five days!" "All bought by the same guy," I asked? "Yep!" Yes, that's a red flag.

Matthew Kramer, that's the guy that bought all of the guns in New Hampshire. That may or may not be a problem. We may not have done a preliminary investigation and looked into the matter if it weren't for the fact that Matthew Kramer's motor vehicle record showed him as a New Hampshire resident AND a Massachusetts resident. He had two valid driver's licenses in the system – one in New Hampshire and one in Massachusetts. That's a problem! You cannot possess more than one driver's license issued by any state – it's illegal. That was the deciding factor for Brian and me to open an investigation into Matthew Kramer's multiple firearms purchases.

Chapter 17
The Bad Actor

Behind every successful fortune,
there is a crime.

~ Mario Puzo

Who was Matthew Kramer? We need to dive into his past and look at what he's recently done to answer this question. I learned through my investigation that Kramer had been arrested in Somerville, MA, in 2007 and was charged with Armed Robbery and the Illegal Possession of a Firearm. Ironically, I had previously investigated that case when I only had about a year or two in my position as a Somerville police detective. I also discovered that Kramer met a kid from New Hampshire on social media and paid him $500.00 to put Kramer on his residential lease. In the eyes of the New Hampshire Division of Motor Vehicles, that's good enough to prove residency and allow you to get a New Hampshire driver's license.

Massachusetts law requires people to have a Firearm Identification (FID) card or License to Carry to purchase a firearm. Those licenses are issued by municipal police departments in the state of Massachusetts. Because Kramer was a convicted felon and a prohibited possessor, he could not obtain a firearms license. So, Kramer took advantage of a loophole in New Hampshire state law to get guns and sell them at a profit.

There is no minimum age in New Hampshire for possessing a firearm. The state's Constitution protects the right to keep and bear arms. You don't need a license to purchase a gun in New Hampshire and are not required to register a firearm. New Hampshire also does not require a waiting period before finalizing a gun purchase. However, you must be a resident of New Hampshire and show identification proving residency to make a gun purchase. So, do the math. Kramer would buy the guns in New Hampshire and bring them across state lines into Massachusetts to sell. A records search revealed that Matthew made his first gun purchase in New Hampshire within an hour of obtaining his New Hampshire driver's license.

The Ruse

Brian and I knew we had to interview this guy, Kramer. But we didn't want to spook him and cause him to run. So, we formulated a plan – a ruse to get him to come to the station. After reviewing some police reports in our database, I discovered that Kramer was involved in an incident at a party several months earlier where he was stabbed in the shoulder. He was unable to provide any suspect information at that time. So, I picked up the phone and called the number we had on file for him. After a few rings, someone answered, "Hello?" "Is this Matthew," I asked? "Yes." "Matthew, this is Detective Oliveira from the Somerville Police Department. Don't worry; you're not in trouble or anything. I'm just doing some follow-up on that incident in which you were stabbed. We may have identified the suspect, and I was wondering if you could come to the station and answer some questions for me?" "Oh, yeah, sure," he replied. Yes! That went well. He agreed to come in the following day.

On October 19, 2010, Brian and I were at the Somerville Police building on Washington Street waiting for Matthew to arrive. He said he'd be there at 3:00 pm, but it was already 3:05 pm, and he hadn't shown yet. *Great, was he dodging us,* I wondered? Brian and I watched the front parking lot from the glass doors at the station, hoping to see him pull into the lot. We knew he drove a red Honda Accord and were watching for that vehicle. Then it happened. We saw Matthew in his red Accord cruising in front of the station. But he drove by really slowly and kept going. Then he circled back, drove by again, and turned on Rossmore Street. *That's weird,* I thought. There were plenty of parking spaces available in the front lot, and he drove right by. Just then, I saw Matthew walking towards the police station from Rossmore Street. I met him at the front door and escorted him into an interview room where Brian had gone to wait for us.

I began the interview with Matthew but introduced Brian as my partner. I didn't want to tell the kid Brian Hudson was actually a federal ATF agent. So, we made small talk and started talking about the car stabbing. Then I sprung it on him, "We're actually here to talk to you about some guns you purchased in New Hampshire. And by the way, my partner is a special agent with the ATF." Boom – there it was! Kramer turned about five shades of white in his face. He sunk further down into his seat and looked like he was going to crap his pants, which I really hoped he wouldn't do at that moment.

Initially, Kramer told us that he was a resident of Massachusetts but later handed me a driver's license from New Hampshire. When I started questioning him about his residency and driver's status, he got all tripped up. He recognized he was in a jam and finally asked, "I'm screwed, aren't I?" When I explained to him that he was looking at possible time in a federal penitentiary for illegal gun purchasing and sales, he asked Brian and me what he could do to help himself. He ultimately confessed to obtaining the New Hampshire driver's license under false pretenses so that he could unlawfully purchase guns.

Matthew stated that he had sold eight of the ten handguns purchased in New Hampshire to an individual named *"Dreddy"* from Boston. He knew the guns were going into the hands of violent criminal street gang members of the Castlegate Gang in Roxbury, Massachusetts. Matthew also said the guns no longer had serial numbers on them because he had used a *Dremel* tool to obliterate them by grinding the serial numbers off. Matthew told us the two remaining handguns were in the trunk of his car that he had parked on Rossmore Street. I asked him if that was the reason, he didn't park in the parking lot of the police station. "Yeah," he said.

Matthew spelled out his whole *business plan* for us and confessed to having committed multiple felonies. In turn, I spelled out for him what would probably happen to him if he didn't help us get the guns from the bad people, he sold them to. Finally, Matthew agreed to work with us. He signed a Consent to Search Form, and Brian and I retrieved a loaded .40 caliber pistol and a loaded 9mm handgun from his trunk. We booked those items into evidence.

We asked Matthew to make a consensually monitored one-party telephone call to *Dreddy* to set up a gun buy for the following day, which he did. After that, we would gather our team, write an operations plan, and prepare to hit and take down members of the Castlegate Gang the next day. Finally, Brian and I cut Matthew loose and told him we would link up with him in the morning. He seemed relieved and couldn't wait to exit the police station. It was a long day.

The next day, Kramer withdrew his cooperation by refusing to return phone calls to investigators and was now on the run. We had federal warrants issued for Kramer's arrest, and we made it our quest to find him.

Some of the guns Matthew Kramer was buying for gang
members around the Boston area.

An undisclosed Castlegate Gang member
displaying his "wares."

Chapter 18
The Doctor

In nothing do men more nearly approach the gods than in giving health to men.

~ Cicero

The foreword of this book speaks of another key figure who is a part of this story. It is vital to introduce him now so that when the time comes to read about how his path intersected with Mario's path, you, the reader, fully understands who this man is and how he came to become acquainted with Mario. So, let's start from the beginning of his life in Rhode Island.

David R. King grew up in Woonsocket, Rhode Island. He was born into a middle-class family in 1973 and is the son of Rich and Nancy King. His dad worked as the superintendent for the Highway Department in Woonsocket and was in charge of snow removal during the winter months. Rich was easygoing but had an intolerance for rudeness and laziness. His mother worked in the actuarial department for Amica Mutual Insurance and shared in dishing out discipline when David stepped out of line.

David had a pretty "normal" childhood. The family lived next to a wooded area where he built forts, played army, shot his BB gun, climbed "and fell" out of trees. David attended the Mount Saint Charles Academy, a private Catholic junior-senior high school that operates through the tradition of the Brothers of the Sacred Heart. Because sending your kid to private school isn't cheap, Rich and Nancy King picked up second jobs so that David could have what they considered to be a better high school education. Rich went to work as a manager for a country club located just across the state line in North Attleborough, Massachusetts, while his mom, Nancy, went to work as a cashier at CVS Pharmacy and Drug Store.

David describes himself as "...the skinny kid who dressed funny" while attending high school. He ran cross country in high school and flirted with hockey before that but said he was never good at either one. This statement seemed ironic to me, coming from a man who subsequently became a triathlete in his 30s and still runs in multiple marathons. He said, "Well, I guess I got better with age." David got in trouble a few times for fighting in high school. He said, "When you're the skinny kid who dresses funny, people tend to persecute you. I didn't have the physical mass to be intimidating at that time. But all you have to do is punch a couple of people in the face, and magically they stop bothering you."

David recalls a rash of bicycle thefts that occurred in his neighborhood when he was 13 years old. The

Woonsocket Police Department encouraged people to bring their bikes into the police station to have them registered and have the frames engraved with a registration number. So, David and his pal Tony C. brought their bicycles to the station and registered them. David and Tony were in Cub Scouts together. One day they decided to skip school and go exploring.

David and Tony rode their bikes out into the woods on a pathway located behind Tony's house. They parked the bikes and decided to walk through the brush to see if they could find anything interesting. As the woods thinned out, the two boys popped out behind a house with an aluminum shed in the backyard. The pair decided to use the shed for target practice. But since they didn't have their BB guns, they used the next best thing – rocks! Yes, they lobbed rocks as hard as they could. The most incredible part in the minds of the teenage youth was the sound the shed made upon impact with the rocks!

This activity lasted a couple of minutes, and the boys were having a ball until a fat guy in a white T-shirt emerged from the house and came into the backyard. He began yelling at the boys when David and Tony decided they'd better scram. To their dismay, they walked back to where they had left their bicycles, but the bikes were gone! As their youthful minds were calculating a plan and what to tell their parents, they ultimately decided to start walking home. They would say to their parents that their bikes were stolen and leave it at that.

As David and Tony walked through their neighborhood, a Woonsocket police car approached them slowly. The officer pulled up alongside the boys, and he asked, "Do you know who these bikes belong to?" The boys looked in the half-open trunk of the police car and saw their bicycles in the back. The boys shook their heads and replied, "No, sir." The officer said, "Well, okay," and drove away slowly. He circled the block and came around again. Finally, he stopped in front of the boys and got out of the patrol car, at which time he asked, "Do you know David King and Tony C.?" The boys answered, "That's us!" The officer responded by saying, "That's funny, these bikes do belong to you!" Then the two teenagers remembered that they had their bicycles registered at the police station – Oops!

The boys were handcuffed and placed in the backseat of the police car. They and their bicycles were driven to the police station, where their parents were called and notified of the situation. The officer escorted David down a hallway, and they stopped in front of an office that had a placard on the door which read, CHIEF of POLICE. At that time, the fat guy in the white T-shirt from the house with the shed came out of the office and made eye contact with David. That was the moment David had a revelation and thought to himself; *I can't believe I pelted the police chief's shed with rocks!* Folks, you can't make this stuff up.

Tony's parents came to the police station. They took Tony away and left David to fend for himself. As David was sweating it out and having thoughts about what his parents would do to him, his father walked into the station. After talking to the officer and getting the blow-by-blow account of what occurred in suburban Woonsocket, Mr. King gathered his wayward son, and they got in the car. After a few minutes of awkward silence, Mr. King told David, "Just so we're clear – this will never happen again, and we're never to speak of this!" David and his dad hadn't spoken of "the incident" for decades.

While attending high school, David began volunteering with his local volunteer fire department. He went to training in the evenings to become an emergency medical technician (EMT) while attending high school during the day. Once he was certified as an EMT in the state of Rhode Island, he was able to go on medical aid calls with the fire department. David developed a genuine love for medical science and for helping people while serving as an EMT.

After he graduated from high school, David and his best friend, Dan, decided they would have careers as engineers, and both applied for undergraduate engineering studies at the Florida Institute of Technology in Melbourne, Florida. Their grand plan was to go into business together as engineers after college graduation. They were to name their company "D & D Engineering" – short for Dan and Dave. He continued to work for a local ambulance company in Melbourne to make some extra cash while attending school. In his sophomore year of college, David decided that engineering wasn't his cup of tea. Every time he thought about different career choices, he kept going back to medicine as he reflected on his time as an EMT. At that pivotal point in his life, David changed his major to biology and transferred to the University of Tampa.

While attending the University of Tampa, David really got into music and minored in music performance specializing in chamber music, a form of classical music. He subsequently graduated with an undergraduate degree in biology and was determined to continue his studies in the field of medicine. David applied for and was denied by a multitude of medical schools. Finally, after careful thought and an unquenching desire to ultimately become a medical doctor, David applied to and was accepted by Saint George's University School of Medicine in Grenada – yes, the same medical school that was caught up in the United States invasion of Grenada in 1983. Grenada is a small island country located in the West Indies, lying about 100 miles north of the Venezuelan coast, where the eastern Caribbean Sea meets the northern Atlantic Ocean.

The master plan was for David to do two years of medical school in Granada and to transfer back to a medical school in the United States. David embarked on his journey to Grenada in 1995. By this time, he was married to his first wife, who fully supported his decision to become a doctor and moved to Grenada with him, along with their retired seeing-eye dog, Rachel. David had helped train Rachel for a local guide dog school in Florida in the previous year. He received good grades and was an honor student during his time in Granada. After two years of studies, he transferred to the University of Miami-Miller School of Medicine in 1997.

David King graduated from medical school in 2000 and is now called "Doctor King." He was a junior resident at Beth Israel Deaconess Medical Center in Boston and completed his senior residency at Jackson Memorial Hospital in Miami. David specializes in trauma, emergency surgery, and surgical critical care. One can also say that Doctor David King thrives on the challenge of operating on the most critical of patients and the adrenaline rush associated with such a challenge. He went on to complete additional subspecialized fellowship training in trauma surgery and surgical critical care.

David was hired as an attending physician at Massachusetts General Hospital in Boston, commonly referred to as "Mass General." Because Mass General is a teaching hospital of Harvard

Medical School, David was subsequently accepted and hired as an assistant professor of surgery at Harvard University and subsequently promoted to associate professor of surgery. These couple of chapters aren't meant to be a complete and all-inclusive memorialization of David's life and career. Instead, they are a brief overview and some highlights of the many facets of his life and career.

David has 15 patents to his name for medical devices he invented. He stated that anyone could develop something and get a U.S. patent. However, he is only interested in creating things that are real, useful, and have a commercial purpose. For example, one of his inventions, *ResQ Foam*, rapidly expands inside the body and seals off deep traumatic wounds. The product has tremendous potential for military and civilian practical application. For example, EMTs out in the field treating a gunshot wound could immediately apply the foam to help buy time to get the victim to surgical care, as could a combat medic taking care of casualties high on a remote mountain top.

Previously mentioned is the fact that David is a triathlete and marathon runner. He was a participant in the 2013 Boston Marathon when the domestic terrorist attack at the venue occurred. David finished about an hour before the first bomb went off when he began receiving a bunch of text messages from people wanting to know if everything was all right –

was he ok? He was unaware of the terrorist attack or the extent of the damage or injuries to casualties, but he felt compelled to report to Mass General even though he was off work at the time.

When David arrived in the emergency department at the hospital, he knew in an instant exactly what he was dealing with. He had seen these types of injuries hundreds of times before on the battlefield, which shall be discussed in the following chapter. A characteristic pattern of injuries was associated with some kind of ground-level improvised explosive device (IED). David and his fellow surgeons took care of 43 patients that day and into the early morning hours of the following day. Because of his tenacity and love for his community, David ran in the Boston Marathon the following year.

On June 9, 2019, Boston Red Sox player David "Big Papi" Ortiz was shot and severely wounded while in East Santo Domingo, Dominican Republic. He was treated at a local hospital in the Dominican Republic. However, the extent of his injuries was so severe that he needed a higher level of care and treatment. The Red Sox sent a medical flight the following day to bring Ortiz to Boston so that he could receive further treatment at Mass General. He underwent a second surgery performed by David, who stated that the situation was grave when Ortiz arrived at his hospital. *Big Papi* had a successful surgery and is alive and well today due to the efforts of Dr. David King.

So, why have several chapters of this book been written and dedicated to David King? Where does he fit into the story? I look at it through this lens - Mario Oliveira's experiences and life make for a fantastic story. But there probably wouldn't be such a remarkable story or a Mario any longer if there was no Doctor David King. All will be revealed in the following chapters.

Former Boston Red Sox player
David "Big Papi" Ortiz (L) and Dr. David King (R)

Chapter 19
Soldier-Doctor

The spectacle of a doctor in action among soldiers in equal danger with equal courage, saving lives where all others are taking them, allaying fear where all others are causing it, is one which must always seem glorious, whether to God or men.

~ Winston Churchill

"I've known nothing other than being at war," said David about his tenure in the United States Army Reserve. His grandfather was an army medic in World War II. In fact, David has his grandad's white armband with the red medical cross framed and hanging on a wall in his home. When he was young, David asked his grandfather why he joined the army. The answer to his question was simply, "Because some people can't, and I can. Freedom doesn't come for free." As David morphed into adulthood, he recognized the same obligation his granddad did – "Some people can't, and I can."

David subsequently joined the army reserves, completed the Officer Basic Leadership Course, and was commissioned as a captain on July 26, 2001 – less than two months before the most significant terrorist attack on U.S. soil that occurred on September 11, 2001. Shortly after that, he would be deployed to combat theaters in Iraq and Afghanistan. For the first 10 or 11 years of his Army career, David worked within the arena of conventional military combat medicine while being assigned to forward surgical teams that were deployed out in the field. During this time, he was quickly introduced to the harsh realities and casualties of war.

Many of us have seen the 1970s television show *MASH*. However, it's no surprise that many folks don't know that MASH is an acronym for Mobile Army Surgical Hospital. One of the critical breakthroughs in combat medicine was the MASH groups that were created in the middle of World War II with the purpose of moving surgical care closer to wounded soldiers rather than transporting the wounded back to a fixed hospital that could be located hundreds of miles away from the battlefield. The more modern concept of the forward surgical team provides rapidly deployable, urgent surgical capability and puts the surgeon as close to the fighting as possible to save the lives of extreme casualties until they can be transported to the next higher level of care.

In 2011, while deployed with a forward surgical team, there were U.S. Army Special Operations Forces (SOF) engaged in a nearby mission when one of the operators was critically wounded with a trans pelvic gunshot wound. To clarify some basic military terminology, it should be noted that personnel in the special operations community do not like to be called soldiers, sailors, airmen, or marines. In current times all special operations forces in the U.S. military use the term *operator* to identify who they are and what they do. In getting back to the story, the operator, as mentioned earlier, was brought to the forward surgical team, where David was serving as one of the surgeons.

Multiple casualties were being treated as a result of them being wounded in this hazardous mission. David recruited a SOF medic who arrived with the wounded operator to assist him as he attempted to save the wounded warrior's life. The operator had a trans pelvic gunshot wound, and his prognosis was not good. However, David worked tirelessly and furiously using some educated guesses and yet skilled techniques to stop the bleeding by placing clamps on and around organs that could be considered to be dangerous.

Because of David's speed, skill, and perseverance, he was able to save the operator's life. Apparently, the SOF medic was so impressed with what he had witnessed that he went back and told his commander that what he saw David do was beyond impressive. The medic said he watched David pull off some "amazing ninja shit!" Evidently, the commander listened.

A few months went by, and David received a phone call from a North Carolina area code. He didn't recognize the phone number. But when he answered the call, it turned out to be the commander of an unnamed Army Special Operations unit. The SOF commander told David he learned of what he had done and how he saved one of his men who should have died in all practical terms. The commander asked David to consider "trying out" for his SOF unit and asked him to go through the selection process. As David so simply put it, "You don't seek to join the unit - the unit finds you," and David accepted the commander's offer.

The selection process for the unit is considered to be classified information. However, we can tell you that David had to attend Ranger School, *Jump* (parachute) School, *SERE* (Survival, Evasion, Resistance, and Escape) School, among other very specialized training. It is easier to turn the doctor into an operator than it is to make an operator into a surgeon. Therefore, a physician assigned to a special operations team deploys with and is physically present with his teammates on missions and while engaging enemy combatants. Thus, David has not only saved many operators and other military personnel in the field, but he has actively been under fire and engaged in combat operations.

On an assault of a highly remote target, while utilizing the cover of darkness, in freezing temperatures, and over rough terrain, an Army SOF operator sustained fragmentation injuries from a hand grenade and multiple gunshot wounds to the thorax. As the firefight evolved, the casualty was moved downhill and away from the objective. However, there was additional enemy contact, and the patient had to be moved further away from the threat. Since David was the surgeon assigned to the tactical assault force, he was able to take immediate lifesaving measures in the field along with an SOF medic. Subsequently, the casualty was evacuated from the area and transferred to several different medical facilities. The fact that this soldier is alive and well today is greatly attributed in part to the immediate care he received on the battlefield.

Sgt. Oliver "Ollie" Campbell wasn't expected to survive the massive chest wound he'd taken in southeastern Afghanistan. In January 2016, the 2nd Battalion Army Ranger was hit five times by insurgent gunfire on a night raid. One bullet shattered a rib, sending bone shards into his lungs. Another nicked an artery, flooding his chest cavity with blood. More blood poured from wounds to his right shoulder, collarbone and cheek.

Minutes later, on an army MH-47E special operations combat helicopter, Dr. David King worked feverishly in the dark. Flying at a low altitude, he had to make do with night-vision goggles and no depth perception. He opened up Oliver's chest from the sternum to the left armpit, inserted chest tubes, and drained 2 liters of blood. Realizing repair surgery couldn't wait until they reached Bagram Airfield, he induced cardiac arrest and clamped the hemorrhaging blood vessels long enough to suture them. Then for two endless minutes, he manually massaged Oliver's heart. Finally, with deft finger-flicks, he caused Oliver's heart to beat back to life.

There are countless stories like the ones mentioned throughout David's military career. Having nerves of steel and practicing battlefield surgeries while under fire have made David a better doctor in all areas of his professional life. After his army career is over, David will still have the valuable experience and lessons learned on the battlefield that he puts into practice in the civilian world. This experience became invaluable on the night of November 2, 2010, when Mario ended up in Dr. David King's operating room.

Dr. (COL) David King with undisclosed
Special Operations team.

Dr. (COL) David King at an undisclosed location.

Chapter 20
The Players

If everyone is moving forward together, then success takes care of itself.

~ Henry Ford

Let's transition back to early November 2010, talk about my team members and revisit the question of Matthew Kramer. Where is he? With him *being in the wind,* none of us knew where he was or what he was doing. It was abundantly clear that Matthew didn't want us to know, nor did he want to be found. So, did he skip town altogether, or was he laying low at some crash pad? I feared that he was pulling serious felonies, possibly crimes of violence, to sustain his livelihood.

We searched high and low for this guy, and he was nowhere to be found. I checked his mother's house, known associates, and the usual hangouts that Matthew used to frequent. I kept batting zero, and it was getting frustrating. Finally, I tried to help out the kid by keeping him out of jail, and he disappeared just as quickly as he appeared on that first day that I met him.

I don't know how many hours we spent tracking down Matthew Kramer. My partner Brian had no choice but to tag along since I was the case agent. I had other law enforcement team members putting *feelers* out and trying to help me locate Matthew. One thing I did know was that we obtained a warrant for Matthew's arrest for multiple felony charges, and he was going to jail when we finally did catch up with him.

Of course, you already know about my partner Brian Hudson. But some of the other law enforcers helping with the Matthew Kramer situation was my Detective Bureau Lieutenant from Somerville PD, Joe McCain. At that time, he had 20 years of service with Somerville PD. Joe was kind of a stocky guy with a beard and was *fully sleeved* with tattoos on both arms. He was a scary-looking dude and resembled an outlaw biker, which came in handy for undercover operations.

Joe McCain was a local boy who was born and raised in Somerville. He graduated from Somerville High School and enlisted in the U.S. Marine Corps before becoming one of Somerville's *finest in blue.* He was damned smart, too, graduating with an undergraduate degree in History from the University of Massachusetts-Boston and a Master's degree in Criminal Justice. Joe is one of the most decent human beings I have ever met and was a great cop too. He was the son of Joseph McCain, Sr., who was a career Massachusetts State Trooper. Sadly, Joe Senior was killed in the line of duty in October 2001.

Detective Ernie Nadile was a 30-year cop for the Somerville PD. He was a seasoned investigator with a laidback, unassuming personality and temperament. His nickname was *Major Crimes* because he got all of the significant homicide cases and had an extremely high case clearance rate.

Another 30-year Somerville cop was Sgt. Jerry Reardon. He was a patrol supervisor who was well-liked by his officers and the higher-ups. He was always very supportive but was never a micro-manager. His wife was an officer for the Massachusetts Bay Transit Authority Police. Jerry was on duty the night my life changed forever.

Pictured from left to right: MA Lieutenant Governor Tim Murray, Governor Deval Patrick, Sgt. Jerry Reardon, Lt. Joseph McCain, Mario Oliveira, Detective Ernie Nadile, and ATF Special Agent Brian Hudson.

Chapter 21
November 2nd – the night I died.

No one can confidently say that he
will still be living tomorrow.

~ Euripides

It was a cool and clear November night in Somerville. Aside from the usual light pollution from the urban landscape and city streetlights, I can remember seeing stars in the night sky. It was general election night in the town on November 2nd, and there were a lot of cops working extra duty assignments keeping law and order and the polling stations. I happened to be working on my normal task force assignment that night. Other than the fact that there would be many people on the streets that evening due to the election, I figured it would be a quiet and uneventful shift. I wore civilian attire and had my badge stowed on a neck chain type badge holder underneath my shirt. I usually didn't wear my bulletproof vest as a task force detective like I did when I was on patrol. But, of course, I'd put it on if we were going to serve an arrest warrant or hit a house on a search warrant.

My partner Brian Hudson and I decided to take a drive-by Matthew Kramer's mother's house on Gibbens Street. The kid skipped town, and he didn't even come up as a blip on the radar. He knew he was going to jail if the police contacted him. So, what would the chances be of him actually being in Somerville on election night? As we pulled onto Gibbens Street from Benton Street, we looked and saw Kramer's red Honda Accord parked in front of his mother's house. Holy crap, he's there! Yes, Matt's car was parked in front of his mom's house. I need to set up on the house and throw a plan together – this I did not expect!

I called my lieutenant Joe McCain and Sergeant Jerry Reardon to come over to my location. I told them to meet me on the sidewalk at Gibbens Street and Central Street because Matt Kramer, a wanted felon, was in the area. The plan we ultimately came up with was that when I saw Matt go to his vehicle, I would run up behind him and get him "proned out" on the ground. Then, Brian will come around with our unmarked police car and "bumper lock" Matt's car so he can't get in and drive away. Essentially, bumper locking is putting the front bumper of our police car against the front bumper of Matt's car. My lieutenant and my sergeant were going to be my backup. Then, finally, I will cuff him up and cart him off to jail. *Yep, sounds like a solid plan; let's do it!*

Oh, no! Matt made it to his car before I could get to him. I started running over to him. As soon as he started his car's engine, I opened his car door, grabbed him around his throat, and put my pistol to his head. I visibly displayed my badge over my shirt, and I started giving him commands, "Get out of the car; you're under arrest. Get out of the car!" I noticed that he straightened his legs out and pressed his feet onto the car's floorboard, making it very difficult for me to pull him out of the vehicle. At one point, Matt started repeatedly screaming, "Fucking shoot me!" "Fucking shoot me!" I remember thinking to myself, *shit, I've got to get him out of this car.*

My sergeant ran up to the vehicle on the passenger side of Matt's car and yelled, "Mario!" I looked at him to see what he wanted. But when I looked back down at Matt, all I could see was the blinding light of muzzle flash through the darkness. The sound of gunfire shattered the calmness of the quiet night. I was blown backward and knocked down on my ass onto the asphalt. *Oh, my God! I've been shot,* I thought to myself.

Then the dark street lit up with brilliant flashes of light – a barrage of gunfire. There was a gunfight going on. I did my best to get into the fight. But as I tried to raise my pistol to aim at my assailant, I couldn't get it to move, no matter how hard I tried to get it to budge. That little bastard had shot me in the forearm of my gun hand, and it was totally disabled.

Brian had the foresight to drag me across the street and away from Matt's vehicle so that I wouldn't be in the crossfire. I could hear all of the chaos going on around me. Then I heard Matt's mother shouting, "That's my son, that's my son," and my Lieutenant, Joe McCain, yelling, "Get back in the house!" At that point, I became fully aware that I had been shot and was losing a lot of blood. As I looked up at the stars in the sky, I became so scared. I began to cry but deliberately controlled and slowed down my breathing so that I would not hyperventilate. I needed to minimize the blood flow so that I didn't bleed out that roadside.

At that moment, it was like a switch got flipped in my mind. I went from feeling shear panic into a state of peace. I remembered playing hide and seek and street hockey as a kid on Rush Street. My brain tuned out all of the pandemonium around me and was preparing me to go to a beautiful place. Instead, I thought about my wife, the birth of my son, my parents, and my childhood home. *Tonight would be the night that I die,* I thought.

Chapter 22
Fight or Flight

To survive, you must surrender without giving in, that is to say, fully accept the reality in all its horror and never give up the will to survive. That allows you to quickly adapt to the situation and dedicate yourself to the present moment rather than wallow in denial.

~ Laurence Gonzales

The parasympathetic nervous system controls bodily functions like digestion when a person is at rest. The sympathetic nervous system tells the body to prepare for physical and mental activity and controls the *fight or flight* response to stressful situations. It causes the heart to beat harder and faster and opens the airways for easy breathing. It also temporarily stops digestion so the body can focus on fast action.

I was still in the fight, coupled with moments of temporary peace and wanting to surrender to the impending death that was coming for me. I tried to respond to the ensuing battle, but my gun hand wouldn't work because that wrist had been shot. I tried to get up and get back in the melee even though my partner had dragged me across the street to safety, but I could not stand up. I was losing blood fast. I continued reminding myself, *Mario, slow down your breathing.*

After the gunfight was over and the gun smoke was starting to clear, I could hear sirens in the distance. Matthew lay bleeding in the driver's seat of his bullet-riddled Honda Accord. He succumbed to his injuries as the ambulance crews arrived. The rest of my team had to deal with Matthew's mother and the other people inside the house. That's when Joe McCain came over to me and knelt next to me. I told him, "Joe, I'm dying. Please tell my family I love them." I could hear and understand him saying, "Kid, you're not dying. Stay with me – you're going to be all right."

As the paramedics were tending to me, I saw Joe McCain walk over to the curb, sit down, and put his pistol on the ground in between his legs. He made a phone call, hung his head down, and began to cry. What I didn't know at that time was that he called his wife and told her he had just heard me say my last words and that I was going to die. Joe was traumatized by the events of that night, and he would be haunted by those unwelcomed memories forever – the memories of losing his dad in the line of duty and now this horrific event.

When I was being loaded onto the ambulance, I heard the voice of my deputy chief, Paul Upton, asking the medics, "How does he look?" One of the medics answered, "Honestly, I don't think he's going to make the trip to the hospital." I couldn't believe he said that right in front of me as if I wasn't even there! I was pissed! I wanted to say, "Listen, you dumb ass, I'm right here, and I'm not going anywhere. I'm going to pull through just despite what you said." In retrospect, that whole dialogue gave me even more of a will to survive.

I knew I was hit several times, and I was bleeding. But I didn't realize that I was shot six times – once to my right forearm, three to the gut, and two to my chest. I think I'm glad I didn't know just how severely wounded I really was at that time. We train for situations like this and watch training films about lethal encounters and surviving gunfights. But there is no amount of training or videos you can watch that'll prepare you for something like what happened to me. A total of 62 rounds were fired in the gunfight.

My brother John (the cop) was working that night and heard what was happening. I learned that he had called my mom and told her that I had been shot and that it didn't look good. He asked her to get dressed and get ready because a car was going to come to pick my dad and her up to bring them to the hospital.

Brian Hudson and Ernie Nadile rode with me in the ambulance. One of the paramedics asked me triage questions, like, "What's your name; how many fingers am I holding up; how many children do you have, etc.?" I remember the medic saying something about my two sons, and I remember thinking, *are you screwing with me?* I corrected him and told him I only have one son – not two. But he swore I told him I had two sons. Whatever!

Matthew Kramer's bullet-ridden Honda Accord.

Chapter 23
Mister Toad's Wild Ride!

There are trauma patients you can walk to the operating room with, and there are those you run with. Mario was one of those you run with.

~ Dr. David King

I arrived in the Emergency Department ambulance bay at Massachusetts General Hospital or *Mass General*. When paramedics took me out of the ambulance, I recall the ambulance's back doors being flung open. I saw a long funnel line of uniformed police officers (like a reception line) cheering me on and giving me well wishes as I was whisked into the emergency trauma bay area. As I went through the tunnel of cops, many were tapping me on my legs and shoulders as the medics ran by them. Some said, "Hang in there, brother," and, "We love you, buddy."

I later learned that well over 500 police officers arrived at the hospital and were waiting with my family for over nine hours to hear my fate. In fact, there were so many cops in the hospital trauma area that the hospital police had to close off an area of the hospital just to accommodate everyone. After that, food began to arrive as well as coffee to feed everyone who was waiting along with my family. I only wish that I was able to personally witness this tremendous act of love for the thin blue line!

Now, back to the harsh reality - I was bleeding out. Once inside, I heard chaos coming from all over the area where I lay on the ambulance gurney. I looked up and could see many doctors and nurses feverishly working on me. They were yelling that they needed blood and were using medical terms that I frankly did not understand. At this point, I closed my eyes in disbelief that I was still alive and just needed to fight to get home to my family. Then, suddenly, I opened my eyes and looked up, and everyone that was working on me had disappeared.

I was so scared and wondered where they all went. *Could they have just given up on me*, I asked? I could still hear all the stressful voices in the background. At that time, I saw the silhouette of a person from peripheral vision on my left side. I dropped my head to the left and could see an image of a person just standing there. It was an older female nurse who appeared to be approximately 60 years of age, heavyset, short, and stalky. This nurse wore large rimmed glasses and had her hair pulled back in a tight bun.

She approached me, placed one hand under my head, lifted my head up slightly, and began to caress my forehead with her other hand. All she would say to me was, "You're going to be okay; you're going to be okay." She had the kindest, most soothing voice

I've ever heard. I asked her to put a blanket on me because I felt so cold. I must have been in shock from my injuries, not to mention the fact that they had cut off all my clothes and let me lay there butt naked on the gurney with the air conditioning on. I started to feel warm moments after asking the nurse for a blanket. I never saw her leave my side, nor did I see her place a blanket on me.

Suddenly, I was whisked away down a hospital hallway with doctors and nurses on each side of my bed. Dr. David King led the charge dragging my gurney down the hall, yelling to hold the elevator - "Hold the elevator, we're headed to floor three, OR." At this point, we were taking a corner to make it to the elevator. In rounding the corner, it felt like my gurney was going to tip over, and I was going to fall off. I thought to myself, *these people are going to fucking kill me before I make it to the operating room!* I swear it felt like *Mr. Toad's Wild Ride* at Disneyland!

I recall looking up and seeing the older nurse assisting in putting my gurney upright as she looked at me and smiled. Moments later, we were on the elevator when I heard Dr. King barking orders at the nurses and his trauma team. Dr. King was telling his team members that he needed blood and to fire up the X-ray machine and a host of other things.

Finally, I'm in the operating room. I was laying on the gurney and staring at the ceiling. I knew where I was because I heard them saying I was headed for surgery, and it was much colder up in the OR. The lights were much brighter in there too. As I was staring at the lights, all I could think of was, *will I ever see my family again?* I just wanted to get home to my little boy, Drew, who was only 3 ½ years old at that time. I couldn't leave him behind without a father.

Again, out of my peripheral vision on my left side, I saw a person's silhouette, and it was the older nurse from the emergency department area. For the second time, she walked up to my gurney and placed one hand behind my head, lifted it slightly, and caressed my forehead with her other hand. She kept repeating, "You're going to be okay; you're going to be okay." To which I replied, "Just let me die." I was so tired of fighting to stay alive. I looked into her eyes and said to her in a weak and raspy voice, "Please tell my son I love him and tell my family I fought hard to stay alive for them." She replied, "Oh, no, no, no, you're not going to die. You're going to be okay." That was all I could remember from when I arrived at the hospital until the lights went out in my mind. I slipped into a stage of darkness and what seemed like an eternal abyss.

Chapter 24
The Operation

It is safer to look and see than to wait and see.

~ Sidney Cuthbert Wallace

Usually, the paramedics would call Medical Control in Boston and then reported on a patient's condition while en route to the receiving hospital. The purpose of doing so is to advise the hospital on just how critical a patient is – it's a form of medical triage. If a patient is critical enough to be a *trauma alert,* they would be met by a trauma surgeon, an emergency department doctor, three trainees, an anesthesiologist, a representative from the blood bank, and a pharmacist who could mix all of the drugs that were needed *on the fly.*

In Mario's case, he was declared as a *trauma alert.* The standard process is for the medics to Medical Control. However, the standard protocol was bypassed, which ended up being a very good thing in Mario's case. One of the detective sergeants at the scene of the shooting, Mike Kiely, had the foresight to call the hospital from his cell phone from the scene of the shooting and briefed them on the situation and Mario's condition. That saved precious minutes, and the trauma team was already assembled and waiting for Mario to arrive.

Mario's condition was so grave when he arrived that he had the *face of death*. Trauma center doctors see that look frequently. It's where the patient's skin becomes gray and ashen due to a lack of blood circulation. Usually, what it means is that the patient is either dead or dying. Dr. David King was the receiving trauma doctor. He could tell just by looking at the *death face* present in Mario that he was dying. Mario's blood pressure began to bottom out. He was truly dying, and there was no time to waste. Rather than continuing to assess the damage, it was crucial to get to the operating room. Within minutes of his initial assessment, Dr. King was screaming down the hallway to the third-floor operating room with Mario and the rest of the trauma team. Again, Mario stated he felt like they were going to dump him off of his hospital bed when the team rounded a corner with him. But for the record, Dr. King contentedly said, "We do go pretty fast. But in 25 years of practicing medicine, we haven't tipped over a patient yet."

Mario and the medical team ended up in O.R. # 26, which is the operating room located closest to the elevator. His blood pressure was already extraordinarily low because of the loss of blood. Without quick intervention, Mario would have died.

Dr. King used a scalpel to cut open Mario's abdominal wall to restore at least some minimal blood flow to his brain. Next, Dr. King got his hands on Mario's *mesentery* (a fold of membrane that attaches the intestine to the abdominal wall and holds it in place), which was doing most of the bleeding at that time.

Dr. King was able to restore some blood flow to Mario's brain, at which time his pulse rebounded. However, fifteen minutes into his surgery, as Dr. King was repairing Mario's right, ascending colon, his blood pressure began to bottom out again – it was dangerously low. So, Dr. King decided to cut open Mario's diaphragm so that he could get his hand up into the paracardial space to manually massage Mario's heart to get the blood flowing once again. Unfortunately, there were so many holes in Mario's organs that it was difficult for Dr. King to figure out the bullets' trajectory and just how many organs were damaged.

Mario had three cardiac arrest events – one in the emergency department and two in the operating room. He was in *perior rest*. In layman's terms, Mario was essentially brain dead during those moments. He could not form memories or have any recollection because the blood pressure wasn't high enough to produce any profusion to the brain cells for the neurons to fire up and synapses to occur. Because patients cannot feel pain when they are in perior rest,

Dr. King made the call to perform surgery without initially having anesthesia administered because the anesthesia would almost certainly cause what little blood pressure Mario did have to be non-existent.

As Dr. King operated on Mario, repairing trauma and gunshot wounds to vital organs, the question came up as to whether he should insert a colostomy or just go ahead and try to repair Mario's colon. The textbook answer to the question would be to have a colostomy brought up into the O.R., insert it, and then go back and conduct a subsequent operation in an attempt to repair the colon. But, for reasons still unknown today, Dr. King decided to go ahead and repair Mario's colon. He thought *I think we'll be okay if I just try to fix the colon now*. It turns out that that was the right call to make at that particular moment.

Dr. King used extreme skill, judgment, educated guesses, and some unexplainable phenomena to save Mario's life. The entire surgery lasted nine hours – and it was nine hours of touch and go.

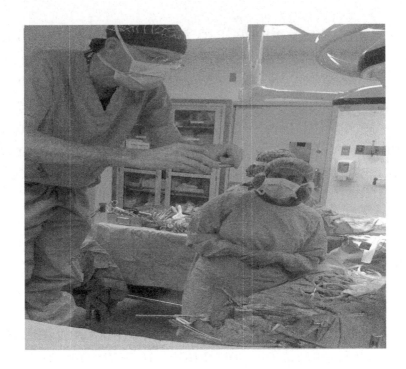

Dr. David King performing surgery
on Detective Mario Oliveira.

Chapter 25
Post-operation

Faith consists in believing what reason cannot.

~ Voltaire

I woke up in the Intensive Care Unit a day and a half after nearly losing my life. My wife Christy and my parents were sitting on some chairs around my hospital bed. I recall looking around the room, unsure as to where I was. I didn't know what day it was or what time it was. I was coming out of a state of disorientation. I thought for sure I was going to wake up in heaven. But instead, I remember being propped up in my hospital bed and seeing a feeding tube going up to my face and into my right nostril. I looked down into my hospital gown and noticed that I had zipper-like staples from my nipple line down past my navel, keeping my stomach together. That's when it dawned on me that I was in bad shape. I knew then that I had pulled off the unthinkable - I survived! But I wondered *what life would be like now; how would I support my family and be able to go back to work; can I still run and do all of the things I could before this happened?*

I began to mumble things to my wife like, "Where the hell am I?" Finally, my wife replied, "You're at Mass General. The doctors saved your life." She fought back the tears as my parents got up from their chairs. They were bawling their eyes out. My mom began to kiss my forehead as my dad held my hand. The nurses working in the Intensive Care Unit overheard us talking and ran to get Dr. King, the man who was responsible for saving my life. Moments later, I saw a tall, slender doctor pull the hospital curtains to the side. He introduced himself as Dr. David King. He asked, "How are you doing, champ?" I replied, "I'm alive; I guess that's a good start."

Dr. King stood at the foot of my hospital bed and reached toward my feet. He squeezed my right foot really hard and asked, "Can you feel me squeezing your foot?" I said," Yeah, I guess I'm not paralyzed." Dr. King said, "You, my friend, are the luckiest S.O.B. I've ever met. You got shot six times at point-blank range, all in your upper torso, and died on me three times. But, I was able to bring you back to life."

My family and I were dumbfounded hearing this revelation. I exclaimed, "What?" Dr. King told me and my family that I had died three times, once in the trauma bay area and twice in the operating room. Dr. King went on to say that one of the times my heart went into cardiac arrest, he cut my diaphragm and reached into my heart with his bare hand and squeezed it back to life. I was completely in disbelief, as was my family. At that point, I began to repeatedly thank Dr. King for his skill and determination to keep me alive.

I asked Dr. King about the older nurse that I had met during my stay at the trauma bay and on my whirlwind ride up to the operating room. I told Dr. King that I wanted to meet this older nurse because she comforted me when I was so scared of dying and leaving my family behind. Dr. King asked me what the nurse looked like. I said, "She was a short, stalky, older nurse wearing circular rimmed glasses, with her hair in a tight bun." Dr. King asked me again where exactly I saw her. I told him a second time that she was speaking with me while I was being treated in the trauma bay and that they ran my gurney down the hallway towards the elevator. I told Dr. King that I saw him pulling my hospital gurney down the hall and repeated verbatim things he said to his trauma team and nurses who were assisting him.

Dr. King looked puzzled when I told him things he said during our trip to the operating room. He told me, "First of all, I absolutely do not have a nurse on my trauma team that looks like the woman you're describing. I know everyone on my team quite well, and I do not have anyone like that...." He stopped and scratched his head. Then he made the time-out signal with his hands and said, "HOLD UP! How in the heck can you remember all these things and be so on point about events when you were clinically dead at that point?" He went on to say, "We were giving you chest compressions and breaths as we feverishly tried to get you to the operating room." Then he said, "Dead people can't form memories!" Dr. King asked me one last time to describe the older nurse, to which I obliged. I could tell that Dr. King was trying to wrap his head around what I was telling him at the moment, but he was having a difficult time with what I had told him. As this conversation continued, my mom collapsed to the floor, crying and holding her face. My dad helped her to her feet and sat her down on a corner chair. My mother could not stop sobbing. I had no clue what the hell was going on at that moment.

I was eventually moved from the ICU to a regular room on the seventh floor and stayed in the hospital for several weeks after my surgery. The nurses removed the staples in my chest on the day I was finally going to be discharged from the hospital. I thought to myself, *man, I don't know if I have healed enough to be released.* But one of the nurses told me I was fine.

When it came time to be discharged, a big press conference was held in front of the hospital. My wife Christy and my mom and dad walked with the nurse and me as I was wheeled downstairs in a wheelchair. The police chief, mayor, and Dr. King were all waiting for me so they could start the press conference. All of the major Boston media networks were covering the event. Although I was happy to be going home finally, I still felt a bit out of it. After the press conference, my family and I were escorted home by a caravan of police vehicles. The support from not only my department but from neighboring law enforcement agencies was amazing.

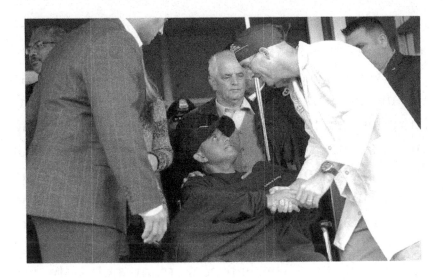

Mario shaking hands with Dr. David King after being
discharged from Mass General Hospital.

Christy and Mario Oliveira being driven home
from the hospital.

Chapter 26
Home, sweet home!

There's no place like home!

~ Dorothy, from The Wizard of Oz

Almost as quickly as I got home, the wound from having my stomach and diaphragm cut busted open, and I began bleeding. My guts literally started to come outside of my stomach area. It was disgusting! Fortunately, some of the cops that escorted me home were still at the house, and they gave me a police escort back to the hospital. It's needless to say that I wasn't happy, but I said it anyway!

The hospital sent me home for the second time and scheduled an aftercare nurse to visit the house to pack my wounds with gauze regularly – basically to keep my guts held inside and prevent any further bleeding. So on my first day back at home the second time around, my aftercare nurse came over to clean my surgery scar and repack it with some gauze. However, the nurse ran out of gauze and needed more. So she asked Christy if there was a drug store nearby. Christy told her there was a CVS not too far from home. So off to the store, Christy went to pick up some more gauze for my visiting nurse.

Shortly after Christy returned home from the drug store, she walked up to me, holding something in her hand. She held out the object she was holding and put it up to my face to see it. In my mind, I was like, *what in the hell is this?* I still had brain fog from physical and emotional trauma. So, my mind wasn't working as sharply or clearly as it usually did. It turns out Christy was holding a pregnancy test up to my face, which had a big plus sign on it! As I previously mentioned, my mind was a bit slow on the uptake, and I thought, *did you cheat on me while I was in the hospital?* Then my brain engaged, and I did the math in my head – I was going to be the father of another child!

It was not a happy time. I had to adjust to being back at home. It was kind of surreal like the shooting didn't happen, but I had the wounds and scars to remind me that it did. I kind of felt like I was in a place that was foreign to me, even though I was back in my own home. I almost felt like a fish out of water, like I didn't know where I belonged or where I fit into the big picture. I suppose that trauma makes one's mind do strange things.

Several days after the revelation of my wife's pregnancy, my mom and dad came over to the house to drop off some soup for us. My mother clutched a picture frame and held it close to her chest. The backside of the picture frame was facing me. She had an intense look on her face. She looked at me and said, "Mario, I want you to put this on your wall – promise me!" I replied, "Of course, Mom, anything you want. I'll do it." At that moment, my mom turned the picture around, and it was facing in my direction as she handed it to me. As I started taking the picture out of her hands, I couldn't believe what I was seeing! All of a sudden, tears began to well up in my eyes. I said, "That's my nurse – that's her!" The picture was a photo of none other than my grandmother, my mom's mother, who had been deceased for at least 25 years.

This is one of the parts where my story gets weird. I found out that when my mom received the phone call from my brother John on the night I was shot, my mother dropped to the floor and began to pray to her mother. We can debate if folks should pray directly to God through Christ or if praying through an intercessory like a saint, which Catholics do, is proper. I am just relaying the facts to you, the readers. It is what it is - my mom fell to her knees and prayed to her mother. Somehow, through some supernatural act of God, my grandmother came to me and comforted me in the hospital.

Do not ask me to make sense of any of these events. I am not God, but I am acutely aware that there is a God. I have come to accept what happened in the hospital after my shooting as a divine act of God that I do not need to understand fully. Acceptance is the key to what eventually would become a happy life for me. But there was still a lot of emotion and trauma to work through during that time. I was finally home and could begin my long road to recovery.

It is crucial to recognize two men who helped my family and me immensely during this time – Chief Mike Cabral and Deputy Chief Paul Upton. Both of these men came to my house every day to check on my welfare. In addition, they always had food in hand for my family and a stuffed animal for my son Drew. The unwavering support and genuine care of one's command staff officers go a long way!

The frame containing a photograph of
Mario's grandmother, Julia Rose Lima.

Chapter 27
Back to Work

Perseverance is the hard work you do after you get tired of doing the hard work you already did.

~ Newt Gingrich

After a few months of staying home and going to physical therapy, I was going out of my mind. There was never a time in my life when I did not work, even as a young kid. After that, I started to feel worthless and useless. I began to lose my way as I had no mission or purpose. At that point, I couldn't even take care of my family the way I wanted to. Now Christy and I were going to have another baby. I felt like I was going off the rails in my mind.

Four months into my recovery, I begged Dr. King to clear me so that I could go back to work. He told me that would not be advisable and wouldn't be a sound medical decision at that time. Nevertheless, I kept working on him every time I went in for a checkup, and I can be pretty convincing. So now, five months into my recovery, I brought up the matter to Dr. King once again, and he stipulated writing a letter to my department allowing me to go back to work. However, there was a caveat that if I even remotely began to feel bad or if I began to suffer any adverse reaction to being shot or the surgery, he was rescinding his letter and having me pulled off of active police duties.

For the first time in five months, other than the fact that God and Dr. King saved my life, I felt like I had just won a significant battle and achieved a considerable victory. Then, a day before I went back to work, I returned to the shooting scene. I was reminded that someone had died there and that I almost died. I spent a few poignant minutes there and just bawled my eyes out. At that point in time, I thanked God for sparing my life. But other than that, I felt an uncontrolled flood of raw emotion – a lot of which made no sense to me at all.

On March 5, 2011, I returned to work only five months after being shot six times. I was ecstatic! I was reunited with my old partners, and a month later, I found myself back on the ATF task force to which I was previously assigned. The Middlesex County District Attorney's Office finally released its findings in a statement to the media, which read in part:

> *"Our investigation further revealed that Matthew Kramer had called an ex-girlfriend in the weeks leading up to*

this incident and told her that he was in
trouble for gun trafficking with the
ATF. He thought he was going to go to
prison for a long time. He also said that
he thought the police were going to
come looking for him, and if they did,
he would get into a shootout with
them."

On July 30, 2011, Christy gave birth to our second son, Tyler David Oliveira. With Tyler's birth, God gave us more joy and hope for a brighter future. He was a gift. Because I was so grateful for Dr. David King, who God used to bring me back to life, I developed a strong bond and friendship with him. Christy and I named our second-born son Tyler David because Dr. King's first name is David. I felt grateful to be able to honor Dr. King in that way.

With the Matthew Kramer matter closed, I could focus my efforts and energy on other cases. For all legal and practical purposes, I could put the Kramer situation to bed; but the fact was that my mind wouldn't allow me to do so. The shooting was gnawing away at me. I had many restless nights because I'd suddenly awaken to muzzle flashes that I saw in my sleep. I'd hear gunfire that wasn't there, except it was there – in the dark corners of my mind.

Waking up in a panic, covered in sweat, and thinking I would die was not a pleasant experience.

In law enforcement, we train on and talk about how not to get into a shooting (de-escalation), how not to get hurt if you're in a shooting, and what happens when you do get into a shooting. We spend very little time as a profession talking about what occurs after you survive a shooting. Before November 2, 2010, I had never been in a shooting and certainly had never been shot. I didn't know how I was supposed to act or feel. But all I knew was that I needed to be back at work with the same people who were there with me when it happened. I also knew that I felt like shit mentally and emotionally. My life was a roller coaster ride of highs and lows – ups and downs.

However, I was working as a cop again, which made me happy. I figured I could get through anything as long as I had my job and my family who supported me through this nightmarish hell on earth. I always wanted to be a cop. So, I guess a big part of my identity was linked to my work.

Chapter 28
Be Careful What You Wish For

Be careful what you wish for, lest it comes true.

~ From Aesop's Fables

I was back to work and glad to be with "my people" once again. But I felt stressed out all of the time. Not a day went by when my office and coworkers didn't remind me of the shooting. Even driving my unmarked police car reminded me of the shooting. It was still fresh and either consciously or subconsciously was always on my mind.

Christy was always worried about me every time I left the house to go to work. My first-born son, Drew, was only four years old by this time. He had extreme separation anxiety every time *his daddy* left the house. He would cry uncontrollably and get sick to his stomach with very severe dry heaves. Sometimes he'd have to straddle the toilet for several hours because he'd actually throw up. It was horrible, and this weighed on me every time I went to work.

This routine continued to go on for eight months until my mind and body couldn't take it anymore. I was stressed out all of the time and didn't feel right like I did before being shot. After work, I'd sometimes do yard work because it relaxed me and helped take my mind off of things only for an hour or two. It was November 2012, one whole year after my shooting. I got off work one evening and decided to rake the leaves in my yard. The change of seasons and Fall on the east coast can keep one pretty busy with leaf control and cleanup.

When I was about halfway through raking, I started having chest pain and shortness of breath. I thought to myself, *that's weird; I must have overworked myself.* So, I went and sat down on the stairs leading up to my back patio deck. I was able to catch my breath, and the pain began to subside as I sat and tried to relax. I went into the house and took a shower. I had some dinner and just chilled for a bit before going to bed. I wasn't tired, so I turned on a rerun of a Boston Celtics game. As I was watching the basketball game, I started to feel the chest pain coming back. It began to intensify and began to generate down my left arm. I knew something was wrong with me, but it was after midnight. Do I try to "soldier through it" and wait until the next day to follow up with my doctor?

Christy was asleep in bed, and so were my two boys. I wasn't about to wake them up to take me to the emergency room. So, I did what any resourceful police detective would do – I called my confidential informant, *Mr. T.* "Hey man, I don't feel right, and I think something bad is going on with me. Can you take me to the hospital?" Mr. T. wasted no time. He came over to my house, loaded me up in his car, and we went speeding off to the hospital. When we pulled up to the rear door of Mass General, I fell out of the car and onto the ground when the passenger side door was opened. I was unconscious, and they hauled me off to the E.R. right away.

Unbeknownst to me at the time, I was hooked up to a balloon pump to keep my ticker going. When I woke up in the Intensive Care Unit the next day. I saw Dr. King standing next to my bed. As I opened my eyes, Dr. King said, "How are you doing, brother?" I asked, "What happened?" Dr. King went on to tell me that I had a massive heart attack and was lucky to be alive. Apparently, I cheated death once again to live another day. I asked Dr. King, "So, you're going to write another letter for me so I can go back to work, right?" Much to my dismay, he replied, "No more letters for you – you're done!" As Dr. King looked over to his right, I also looked in that direction. There was my police chief sitting in the corner of my hospital room. Now the Chief had heard what Dr. King had said to me. *Shit, there's no way the Chief will let me go back to work full-duty after hearing that. I'm so screwed,* I thought.

I stayed at the hospital for another week and was finally discharged. Unfortunately, I was spending way too much time at that place and was having *déjà vu* moments that reminded me of the shooting. Finally, I got home and began my long road to recovery. Rather than explain a long process of paperwork and bureaucracy, I'll simply say that it was well documented my heart attack was related to my job, the trauma I had suffered from the shooting, and the continual stress I was under after returning to work.

I filed for retirement and asked the Chief if he'd put me in for an enhanced retirement under Massachusetts special legislation that allows injured police officers to receive more retirement compensation if the requested retirement was a direct result of being severely or gravely injured on the job. Without reservation, he applied for it and told me, "Mario, you earned it. Unfortunately, you earned it the hard way." Now the next thing to occur would be for the city, in other words, the Mayor, to sign off on the enhanced retirement package. Except he didn't! I was administratively betrayed not by my department but by a stuffed-shirt, political, desk-riding Pogue who was trying to look like he was saving the city money in an election year.

Chapter 29
A Deep Dive into Depression

*A big part of depression is feeling really lonely,
even if you're in a room full of a million people.*

~ Lilly Singh

I was no longer a cop, and my special legislative retirement hadn't come through. I started losing weight like crazy. I didn't want to eat; I couldn't sleep; I didn't want to be around people, not even my own family. What kind of man had I become. I had no place to go every day except my home, where I stayed locked away from everybody and everything. I stayed in my dark bedroom and with my dark thoughts.

It was bad enough to have post-traumatic stress and reoccurring nightmares. But now, this was something else. At least with a mission and purpose in life, I had the will to push through the broken memories and lack of sleep. I went from going back to work – to having a heart attack – to being unemployed and receiving only a partial service retirement. I felt my world coming apart. If I wasn't well enough to work, how could I even figure out another way to support my family.

I used to be so very active. I worked out at the gym all of the time and had the energy to spare after I got off of work. I used to play catch with my eldest son after work and run errands. Now I was just holed up in my room with the television on for *white noise*. I was sad all of the time and lost interest in all of the activities I used to do. I had no energy and was fatigued every day. On the rare occasions when I actually did start to fall asleep, the nightmares would wake me up due to the post-traumatic stress.

The emotional anxiety hurt me almost more than being shot. My department cut off access to my department email, which was one of my only lifelines to the PD. They took away my department-issued firearm, and no one could seem to tell me the status of my pending retirement. Even the deputy chiefs were kept in the dark about my situation. I lost my sense of identity and was no longer a member of the club – the *thin blue line*.

One day I decided I couldn't live like that anymore. I didn't know how I would do it, but I would try to pull myself out of this major slump. So, I began to force myself to get out of bed, even when I did not want to get up. I slowly pushed myself to at least not neglect to do yard work and chores around the house. I started leaving the house and would go places other than my scheduled doctor's appointments. On some occasions, I'd even go to the store and buy groceries. But I surely wasn't ready to run any marathons or anything like that!

My retirement was finally approved on March 1, 2014. At least I could support my family going forward from that day. Christy stuck by me like glue, and I knew I was blessed to have her in my life and by my side. After that, things started getting better as I tried to figure out my new mission and define my purpose in life.

On June 30, 2015, I started my day after briefly talking to my neighbor. I went inside my house and began to take a shower. As I grabbed the soap bar from the built-in soap holder, it slipped out of my hand and fell onto the shower pan floor. I reached down and picked it up, but it slid out of my hand again and dropped onto the floor. When I bent over to pick it up for a second time, it was like someone had turned out the lights. I blacked out and did a face-plant onto the shower floor. If that wasn't bad enough, my leg hit the shower temperature control knob, which put the water on fully HOT.

As I lay getting pummeled by scalding hot water, Christy came running into the bathroom. Fortunately, she heard the loud thud I made as I impacted the shower floor. She turned off the hot water and attempted to wake me up. I became conscious and tried to pick myself up off the floor. However, I couldn't move my whole left side – I was paralyzed! For any of you that are good with diagnosing medical symptoms, you guessed it – I suffered a stroke. Christy dialed 911 on our phone and got another ambulance ride to Mass General of all places.

Just when things started looking up, and now this! I was once again treated by my friend, Dr. David King. He told me that my prognosis was good with a lot of hard work. I was eventually discharged from the hospital and sent home. During the whole summer and fall of 2015, I spent a great deal of time in physical therapy and speech therapy, learning how to walk, talk, make the bed and do the things I used to all over again.

Chapter 30
A New Purpose

Without God, life has no purpose, and without purpose, life has no meaning. Without meaning, life has no significance or hope.

~ Pastor Rick Warren

In 2013, I was down to roughly 145 lbs. soaking wet from being emotionally drained and stressed the hell out worrying about my future and how I was supposed to support my family financially. I was still in limbo with my retirement process and still waiting on an answer from the Mayor of Somerville.

This process took a toll on my mind, body, and soul. I would occasionally attend the mayor's campaign events and write his campaign a check from my already draining personal checking account to show him I was one of his "boys." Sadly, that's the way dirty politics are played. I won't elaborate too much more on this topic as I could write an entirely separate book on dirty politics in my city.

During this very emotional time in my life, I prayed a lot to God and spoke to Him during quiet moments in my room or if I was alone and self-reflecting. I can honestly say that I got the idea and motivation to effectuate positive change during those intimate moments of speaking with God. I knew how much my family and I were suffering from this emotional roller coaster ride that we were on.

I came up with the idea of creating a non-profit organization that morphed into the Violently Injured Police Officers Organization (VIPO). I collaborated with another permanently injured police officer from the City of Woburn. His name is Robert DeNapoli. Bob was shot six times and was permanently injured in the line of duty while responding to an armed robbery of a jewelry store. He, too, battled his city administration for his "special legislation" retirement. Together Bob and I began to do public speaking engagements to raise awareness about this injustice. We also co-authored legislation that would effectively change things in Massachusetts forever. Our legislative bill would guarantee that all future police officers who, God forbid, got shot, stabbed, run over, or violently assaulted by a suspect would receive 100% of their base pay and their respective pay raises. Massachusetts law currently says that any police officer injured in the line of duty would be eligible to earn 72% of their salary (income tax-free). The law further states that any police officer who is retired with "accidental disability" cannot earn more than $15,000 per and/or work more than 1200 hours per year.

However, suppose a police officer dies in the line of duty. In that case, there is a one-time tax-free payout currently at $389,825.00 that is funded through the Public Safety Officer Benefits Program (PSOBP), which the Department of Justice administers. In addition to the Federal payout, the state of Massachusetts has a one-time line of duty death payout of $300,000.00, which is also tax-free. The deceased officer's beneficiary would also receive their loved one's base salary at the rank they held at the time of death for the rest of their life to include any raises or contractual stipends. The deceased officer's beneficiary would also have real estate tax exemption on their primary residence as long as they reside in the state of Massachusetts.

But wait, there's more. First, if the deceased officer's children would like to attend higher education after high school, they would have in-State, fully-paid college tuition. If the officer's children are on a civil service list in Massachusetts, they will go to the top of the list under a wounded veteran. This statute is called a 402A status. Lastly, if the deceased officer is an active member of the National Rifle Association (NRA), the beneficiary would receive a one-time tax-free payout of$35,000.00.

I outlined the differences between benefits afforded to police officers who die in the line of duty and those who survive a critical incident that leaves them permanently injured. Essentially the message is that, financially speaking, your family is better off if you die in the line of duty than if you survive. You effectively get punished for surviving. This revelation has never sat well with me. I have been on a mission since 2013 to effectuate change that would provide permanently injured police officers with 100% of their base pay and allow them to get the raises that they would have received had they not been critically injured as a result. Robert DeNapoli and I started our Violently Injured Police Officers Organization in 2013, and we have flourished ever since. I have assisted in introducing our legislation in 7 different states (Massachusetts, New Hampshire, New Jersey, Georgia, Florida, Colorado, and Arizona). We have passed our legislation (or a similar version thereof) in the states of Kentucky and Oklahoma. My vision from our Almighty God is to take my idea and get every state in the United States to file and pass our legislation which will give much-needed benefits to ALL police officers who are violently and permanently injured in the line of duty.

I firmly believe that God spared my life the night of November 2, 2010, so that I can be his conduit here on earth to spread a message of HOPE & FAITH! I sincerely hope and pray that no matter what troubles or illness you have, God will help you overcome your struggles and lead you to the eternal joy of His light through faith. I desire to exemplify God's light for all who struggle and be the hands and feet of Jesus.

Chapter 31
Reality is Stranger than Fiction

*Face reality as it is, not as it was or
as you wish it to be.*

~ Jack Welch

For Dr. David King, the reality of what happened in the case of Mario was unique. As a pragmatic, thinking man, he believed what Mario had told him did occur. In other words, Mario was telling him the truth. But he didn't understand it. He ran the different possible scenarios through his mind for some sensible explanation as to why Mario was dead but could quote conversations and events that had occurred while he was unconscious and not breathing. How could this be without something extraordinary or supernatural having occurred?

David dismissed what had happened as some weird kind of nonsense. He admittedly said that he didn't have a full appreciation for what had occurred in his operating room the night Mario had been shot. There was no "light bulb" moment when David suddenly came to appreciate the event as anything other than happenstance. After days of reflecting on it, dismissing it, and coming back to it in his mind, he even considered, *hmm, maybe I ought to rethink this whole thing.*

In January 2020 and almost a decade after Mario's shooting, David gave a briefing at the Pentagon in his capacity as a U.S. Army Reserve surgeon and colonel. As he got in front of his audience and began to speak, he felt lightheaded but continued to press on. Then he began to feel dizzy, and his speech became slightly impaired. His word recall ability was diminished, and he had a sense of *brain fog.* This person was not the same laser-focused and sharp Dave King that everyone knew and was used to. David knew something wasn't right with him. But he went back to his hotel and ran 13 miles on a treadmill before flying home to Massachusetts the following day.

Like any good lawyer, it is not advisable to represent yourself in a court case – it is not a great idea for medical doctors to diagnose themself. However, David figured since he was in excellent physical condition as a competitive runner and elite special operations team member, it may have been caused by something in the brain. So, he went to his primary care physician to help him figure out what was going on. David was put through a series of tests, and an MRI of his brain was performed. The MRI results show a possible tumor in the thalamus of David's brain.

This was not good news by any stretch of the imagination. To really know if he had a brain tumor, David would have to wait another eight weeks and have a second MRI of his brain to ascertain if there had been any change in size and growth since the tumor was in a location that was not accessible with a biopsy. After eight weeks had elapsed, David had the second MRI. It revealed that the mass had gotten smaller, which was indicative of a glial cell reaction to a stroke.

A *bubble study* was conducted to determine the root cause of the stroke. A bubble study is a noninvasive test that allows physicians to assess blood flow through the heart. The study ruled out certain factors and pinpointed the problem with David's heart. He had a septal defect between his left and right atrial. With David being relatively young and a runner in excellent condition, it was probable that his intensive physical activity caused the blood to get pushed so hard and fast that the hole in his heart became enlarged. In turn, the hole likely provided an opening for a tiny blood clot to pass from the right to the left side of the heart, which traveled to the brain and caused the stroke.

David subsequently had what would be considered a reasonably routine procedure to close the hole in his heart. It was performed in the catheterization laboratory (cath lab) at Mass General Hospital, where David works. For all intents and purposes, the procedure went well and was a success.

It should be noted that David had previously gone through a divorce with his first wife and was engaged to be married to his fiancé Kym at that time. While David was going through his health challenges, he was also being tested in his relationship with Kym. They had gone through some difficult times and had called off their engagement. David was down in the dumps and feeling just miserable. He was sad, depressed, and lonely.

One morning in August 2020, David walked his dog Fletcher, a springer spaniel. It was a clear, pretty day in Cambridge, Massachusetts. But David was still grieving over the loss of his relationship with Kym. So, in a quiet moment of self-reflection and introspection, David began to talk to God. In his mind, he said *Lord, I'm so sad. If this is all there is, just take me down now.* Little did he know at the time just how profound his words were and that his silent prayer would be tested just a few hours later. David and Fletcher finished their walk, and David got ready to head out for work.

It was *trauma fellow* graduation day at Mass General, and David was the Trauma Surgery Fellowship Program director. The Trauma Fellowship is a two-year program designed to prepare a surgeon for a career in traumatology and post-traumatic reconstructive surgery. As the head of the program, David would present the graduate with a beautiful chrome machete with their name engraved on the blade, a tradition he had started many years earlier. So, he was lugging a machete around in his backpack when he arrived at the hospital.

During David's shift, he began to feel out of sorts. He ended up getting extremely light-headed to the point of passing out. Something was very wrong – there was a complication with the heart procedure that was previously done, and he thought there might be something unexpected going wrong. One of his colleagues insisted that he be sent across the parking lot to the surgery center in a wheelchair. But David being David, said, "No way! I'll walk to the surgery center and sit in a wheelchair when I get to the back door." So that's precisely what he did.

David was admitted to the hospital for continuous cardiac monitoring under the care of his performance cardiologist, a cardiologist who specializes in taking care of athletic hearts. Since this was supposed to be Fellow graduation day, David called the junior doctor up to his hospital room to shake his hand and present him with his ceremonial machete. But, as he watched his monitors, he could clearly see that something wasn't right in his chest. He was going into rapid atrial fibrillation, which soon decayed into ventricular tachycardia (v-tach) to the point in which his heart went into a fatal arrhythmia. David obviously recognized the symptoms that he was dying. As he began to slip into the abyss, David recalls reaching out towards his estranged fiancé, Kym, with his left hand. The harder he tried to reach for her, she moved further away. But, of course, she wasn't really in the room.

The darkness came, and then came the abysmal light. David said he felt like God was shaking him by the shirt and saying something to the effect of, "Come find me or come find your way back to me." David was acutely aware of the presence of God and felt as if God was allowing him an opportunity to do things over again. David subsequently became conscious following an emergency electrical shock to his heart and is now alive and well. Finally, he understands what Mario had experienced on the night of November 2, 2010.

Chapter 32
The Three Amigos

I do believe we're all connected. I do believe in
positive energy. I do believe in the power of prayer.
I do believe in putting good out into the world. And
I believe in taking care of each other.

~ Harvey Fierstein

We seem to live in such a finite world. Because of this factor, it is sometimes difficult to see the forest through the trees and truly know there is more than meets the eye. Generally speaking, people live in a micro-paradigm where their world-view is narrow and limited by their own lack of grasping the fact that this blue sphere we are a part of is just a speck in a greater universe.

I believe that God brings people together for a greater purpose. We are all inter-connected because of our humanity. For me (Keith Knotek), I grew up in California and was raised in a traditional Christian home. I received my *religious education* and tried to be a good guy. But that's as far as it went. I lived my life according to my rules which were based loosely on how I was raised and more so on my own will and desires.

I went into law enforcement at a very young age and quickly began to be exposed to the *real world*, in which everything was not all rainbows and unicorns. Bad things happen to good people all of the time. I became less trusting of others and more self-reliant with each passing day. Over a 30-year career, I saw things that one cannot unsee. I lost count of the homicides and horrific traffic accidents I dealt with frequently. I saw dead children and entire families wiped out due to murder-suicide. I was constantly exposed to *the evil that men do*. Unfortunately, I am not unique because this is the sad reality for many police officers.

However, I may be unique because I should be dead several times over. However, God saw fit to keep me around for a bigger purpose than just me and my own selfish desires. I've been in a few knockdown drag-out fights; several shootings – one in which one of my deputies was shot and killed and had a lunatic try to rip my gun out of my own holster so that he could try to use it against me. I've been pinned down by gunfire for over an hour. But I'm still here!

Like so many guardians and protectors, I couldn't handle the mental strain and anguish of the daily grind. I went through periods of depression which I denied even when my wife could see it. Because of the negative stigma in the public safety community regarding seeking mental health help, I did what many of the *old-timer* cops did – I drank. I drank in private to numb the pain I had to deal with in public. I began to isolate myself and didn't want to be around people. So, I let post-traumatic stress consume my life for a long time. Yes, I still went to work and fulfilled my responsibilities. But I did so with a hidden face and a fake smile. I suffered in silence which is an all-too-common theme in the first-responder world.

I began to self-implode to the point where I realized something had to change. In May 2019, I was at my lowest point. I wasn't dead; however, I was mentally broken and spiritually dead. I was asleep one night when I was awakened by something or someone in the wee hours of the morning. I opened my eyes, looked over to my right, and saw a figure standing next to my bed. I was not afraid, but I didn't know who or what I was looking at. He or they didn't say anything to me but instead communicated with me non-verbally. It conveyed a message of peace and hope to me – hope for the future. I know what you're thinking – *this guy is nuts*. I know it's hard to believe, but that's what happened.

I rolled over and went back to sleep. In fact, I got the best sleep that night that I've ever had in my entire adult life. When I woke up in the morning, I had clarity. Of course, I didn't understand it. But I felt different somehow like I knew how to fix all of my problems. All of my character defects became known to me, and I became aware of the presence of God in my life from that point on. Everything began to change for me in a good way. Did I see God? I don't know what I saw, but I know that it was of God and was good.

I began to become self-aware and had peace in my life. I also discovered the *Four Pillars of Resilience* which has to do with paying attention to and nurturing the mental, spiritual, physical, and social components of life. It is a holistic approach to living a healthy, balanced, and happy life. I renewed my faith by tapping into the spiritual part connecting with God daily through prayer and getting back to my Christian roots. I got help for the post-traumatic stress issues and stopped drinking alcoholic beverages. Life is good! Because I got help, made lifestyle changes, and lived life according to God's will and now my own, I can participate in and do things I never thought possible.

Mario Oliveira was an immigrant kid who came to the United States at the age of four. He realized his boyhood dream of becoming a police officer, only to get shot six times thirteen years into his career. He, too, saw and experienced the evil that men do. But Mario died and was brought back to life through divine providence. He had a spiritual, supernatural experience that transcended anything that is known in this ordinary world.

His road to recovery was not an easy one. Mario also suffered from post-traumatic stress, depression, and not having a purpose to fulfill. So, he did what most people do under those circumstances. He checked out from society, self-isolated, and withdrew from everything he used to enjoy doing. As a result, he lost a bunch of weight and felt miserable.

During his personal time alone with God, he finally realized his new purpose in life – to fight for severely wounded police officers who are permanently disabled. He started a non-profit organization to help injured officers and their families and subsequently went back to work training and teaching officers in technical aspects of law enforcement.

Enter David King, a skilled surgeon, U.S. Army Reserve colonel assigned to an elite special operations unit, associate professor of surgery for Harvard Medical School, and an inventor of medical devices. He did not know Mario until that fateful night in November 2010, when God used him to save Mario's life.

David did not understand how a nurse that wasn't on his surgical team could be in the room with the group of people. Yet, the only person who saw her was Mario. This was outside the realm of possibilities. But David kept going back to the situation and running all of the circumstances through his mind to find some plausible explanation for what had happened.

As a man who struggled with his faith after the evil and carnage he witnessed on the battlefield, it seemed to him that there was no God at times. It wasn't until a decade later, when he had his own personal experience with death, that he began to understand there is more to this scientific and empirical world. Yes, David now has an appreciation for God, miracles, and extraordinary things. He died as Mario had died and also had a spiritual experience when his heart went into a lethal rhythm. David watched himself decay as he slipped into unconsciousness. Finally, he died, was visited by God, and was given a second chance at living his earthly life.

Collectively, all three of us men had experienced trauma in our lives, had spiritual experiences that cannot be explained in earthly terms, and stepped out into the light. We have discovered there is more to life than meets the eye on the surface. We had to dive deep into the darkness to find the light that led us to discover our purpose in life.

I believe that God puts people in our lives for a purpose. He uses others to help carry out His mission and purpose. Therefore, we are stronger together as a group of individuals working together collectively for a cause than going it alone. There is no doubt God connected Mario, David, and me for a purpose. So, he brought us together to tell the fantastic story of life, death, faith, and living with purpose.

I wasn't looking to write another book, nor was I looking to obtain another friend. But out of the blue, I was blessed to be able to tell this story so that others may have hope, AND not only did I find another friend, I now have two more companions whose friendship shall stand the test of time. Getting this true story out to the public has been a long time coming, but it is now the right time for people to have renewed hope for their future.

Conclusion

After nearing the end of this book, I'm sure one of the looming questions is why God revealed himself to these men in such a manner? Why do some people have spiritual experiences while others do not? We are not God, and we do not know the answer to this very perplexing question. God sent Mario the spirit of his deceased grandmother to comfort him in his time of need. That is what Mario needed on his death bed to turn this story around for God's glory. We cannot make supernatural events occur as mere mortals, but God can, and He does, even today. Mario's experience answers the question, where do my loved ones go when they die?

Dr. David King sums it up best by saying, "God creates miracles that maybe aren't as biblical as we want them to be. Maybe God isn't parting seas and feeding masses in the ways we can read in scripture. Maybe He saved Mario simply so that he could meet his unborn son." David and Mario are alive and well today. They both get to do things over again in their earthly life with the full knowledge that there is a loving, omnipotent God who has their well-being at heart.

God touched me very personally when I was on the brink of self-destruction. He sent a spiritual presence to convey a message of hope, peace, and recovery to me personally. As a result, I chose to live my life for God and turn from my selfish ways from that point on. I decided to do the right things for the right reasons, and my life has been blessed because of it.

Today, Dr. King is a *"full-bird"* colonel (O-6) in the Army Reserve and is assigned to U.S. Special Operations Command. He still works as a trauma center surgeon at Mass General and is currently an Associate Professor of Surgery at Harvard Medical School. Dave enjoys competing in marathons, triathlons, and shooting. In addition, he appreciates the outdoors and finds solace in camping and hiking. Dave has two teenage daughters and is now married to his wife, Kym. They reside in the Cambridge area with their dog Fletcher.

Mario Oliveira works as a law enforcement coordinator for the New England State Police Information Network (NESPIN) in the Eastern Massachusetts Metro/Boston area. He plans and coordinates liaison functions with local and state police agencies. Although he still has the physical scars from being shot, he has healed mentally and emotionally from the trauma he suffered. As a result, his mission and purpose are to tell his story to various audiences to give them hope, faith, and a will to survive the unthinkable. Furthermore, Mario's vision is to have his model 100% disability retirement filed in every state in the United States to give protection to all his brothers and sisters in blue who are permanently injured as a result of a violent assault.

After reading this book, we desire that you find peace, solace, and hope for the future. When life gets to be too much, and you feel like you're at the end of your rope, please remember there is life after trauma. There is one who has the power to calm the storm – a power greater than yourself.

Mario, Christy, Drew, Tyler David, and Luke Oliveira.

About the Authors

Mario L. Oliveira

Mario Oliveira is a retired Police Detective from the Somerville, Massachusetts Police Department. He was shot in the line of duty, died, and was brought back to life on November 2, 2010. Mario subsequently started a non-profit organi-zation, the Violently Injured Police Officers Organization (VIPO), and has dedicated his life to ensuring that other officers and their families have the resources they need when a law enforcement officer is killed or violently injured in the line of duty. He also serves as the New England Chapter of Concerns of Police Survivors (COPS) president.

Mario received an Honorary BS in Criminal Justice from Fisher College, in which a scholarship in his name was founded. He is the most highly decorated police officer in the history of the Somerville Police Department. Mario resides in Tewksbury, Massachusetts, with his wife Christy and their three sons.

Keith R. Knotek

Keith Knotek is a retired sheriff's sergeant and police commander with thirty years of law enforcement experience in California. Keith has written several books, including *From Sorrow to Amazing Grace: One Cop's Journey*, which was turned into a movie titled *One Cop's Journey* in 2022.

Keith is a graduate of the FBI Law Enforcement Executive Development Association Regional Command College, the California POST Executive Course, the California POST Sherman Block Supervisory Institute, and holds an MA in Organizational Leadership and a BS in Criminal Justice. He is an adjunct university instructor and lectures on topics related to mental health, resilience, and law enforcement. Keith is an Advisory Board member for the Violently Injured Police Officers Organization (VIPO) and enjoys volunteering, boating, and fishing. He lives in Prescott, Arizona, with his wife, Lily, and has two adult daughters.

Made in United States
North Haven, CT
07 June 2022

19959084R00124